STAR WARS
THE CLONE WARS
REPUBLIC HEROES

PRIMA Official Game Guide

Written by:

Fernando Bueno

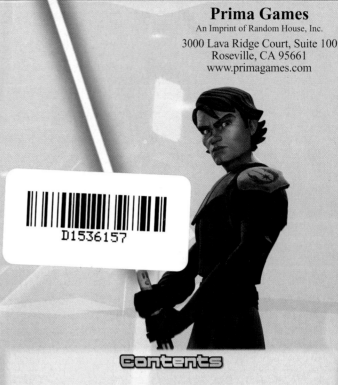

Prima Games
An Imprint of Random House, Inc.

3000 Lava Ridge Court, Suite 100
Roseville, CA 95661
www.primagames.com

D1536157

Senior Product Marketing Manager: Donato Tica
Associate Product Manager: John Browning
Manufacturing: The "S" Team
Design and Layout: Bryan Neff & Jody Seltzer
Copyeditor: Carrie Andrews

A very special thanks to: Paul Armatta, Cristopher Lee, Xavier Rodriguez, Stephen Ervin, Brandon Cox, Virginia Villarreal, Robert Valentine Tameem Amini and Gavin Leung.

Important:
Prima Games has made every effort to determine that the information contained in this book is accurate. However, the publisher makes no warranty, either expressed or implied, as to the accuracy, effectiveness, or completeness of the material in this book; nor does the publisher assume liability for damages, either incidental or consequential, that may result from using the information in this book. The publisher cannot provide any additional information or support regarding gameplay, hints and strategies, or problems with hardware or software. Such questions should be directed to the support numbers provided by the game and/or device manufacturers as set forth in their documentation. Some game tricks require precise timing and may require repeated attempts before the desired result is achieved.

ISBN: 978-0-307-46557-3
Library of Congress Catalog Card Number: 2009907701
Printed in the United States of America

08 09 10 11 LL 10 9 8 7 6 5 4 3 2 1

Contents

About the Author

Fernando "Red Star" Bueno (aka dukkhah) has been a gamer since opening his first Atari, and has been writing creatively since his early years in high school. During college he combined his loves for gaming and writing and began freelancing for popular gaming websites. The San Diego native found his way to Northern California shortly after high school. After graduating from the University of California, Davis, with a dual degree in English and art history, he was able to land a job as an editor for Prima Games. Though happy with his position as an editor, his life called him to Las Vegas where he now resides. During the move to Nevada, he also made the move to author and has since written a number of game books, including *Naruto Uzumaki Chronicles 2*, *Prince of Persia: Two Thrones*, *Fight Night Round 3*, and *Stubbs the Zombie*.

In his time off he enjoys the works of Hermann Hesse, Johann Van Goethe, Franz Kafka, and EGM. When not writing for Prima, he continues to work on his craft as a poet.

We want to hear from you! E-mail comments and feedback to fbueno@primagames.com.

INTRODUCTION

Acknowledgments

It has been a while since I last worked with my good friend Don Tica. It's always nice to work on a project with him. I can't imagine working with a more supportive product manager than him. And it's been even longer since I've worked with John Browning. If there is a more laid-back editor, I've yet to meet him or her. Thanks for being such a great team to work with. You both made this a stress-free project.

Of course, I would never have gotten this book done without the myriad of people at LucasArts. Thank you to Brandon Cox, Tameem Amini, Christopher Lee, Robert Valentine, and Xavier Rodriguez for providing me with a great deal of information. Thanks, of course, to the rest of the people who spent countless hours making sure we had everything we needed, from hints, item locations, and art to answering questions and providing updated builds on a regular basis.

Finally, thanks to my lovely Leslie for being so supportive and easing my stress level with every passing day.

The Story up Until Now...

Surely you've come to know the story of Anakin Skywalker, Jedi Master Yoda, Obi-Wan Kenobi, and the Jedi Order. You may even be familiar with the story of the Rebellion against the Empire or have heard whisperings of a dark organization named the Sith. But for those who need a reminder of where it all began, the following section provides all the background information needed to begin your adventure as you enlist in the Clone Wars.

Star Wars: Episode I–The Phantom Menace

During a time of turmoil in the Galactic Republic, a powerful organization known as the Trade Federation engaged in an aggressive maneuver to block trade routes to and from the planet Naboo.

While the Congress of the Republic stalled on resolving the conflict, the Supreme Chancellor of the Republic secretly sent out two Jedi Knights to help resolve the issue quickly and quietly. Unfortunately, both the Jedi Knights and the people of Naboo were unaware that the Trade Federation was being secretly coerced into their actions by a more powerful dark force.

Upon arriving to meet with the Trade Federation delegates, the Jedi were ambushed and forced to flee. In their escape, they rescued Queen Amidala of Naboo and made a dash across the stars. As they fled, Qui-Gon Jinn, the elder of the two Jedi, came upon a small child with an extraordinarily high capacity for the Force—the energy that flows through all living things and that Jedi can harness into unique abilities. Convinced that the child, Anakin Skywalker, was the one prophesied to bring balance to the Force, Qui-Gon Jinn rescued him from slavery and took him on as an apprentice. It was not until after they met with the Jedi Council that Anakin's dark and troubled past was brought into question. Unmoved by the Council's warnings, Qui-Gon Jinn continued informally with Anakin's training.

As the Jedi fled from the Trade Federation with Queen Amidala, they found that they were being hunted by a dark figure highly skilled with a lightsaber and shrouded in the dark side of the Force. Upon hearing of the mysterious figure's attack on Qui-Gon Jinn, the Jedi Order realized that the Sith—a dark Order long thought to be extinct—was actually still active. Meanwhile, Senator Palpatine, a two-faced politician with dark ambitions, secretly and successfully schemed to overthrow the Supreme Chancellor and took his place.

In a final move of desperation, Senator Amidala (accompanied by Qui-Gon Jinn, Obi-Wan Kenobi, and Anakin Skywalker) fled back to Naboo to help liberate her planet from the Trade Federation. Though they were supposed to protect Amidala, the Jedi had a second motive for returning. They were to draw out the Dark Lord who attacked them earlier and reveal the existence of the Sith. In a final confrontation, Qui-Gon Jinn exposed but was defeated by the Sith Lord Darth Maul, who was in turn defeated by Obi-Wan Kenobi. In the end, Palpatine became the new Supreme Chancellor and took control of the Republic, Naboo was liberated from the Trade Federation, Obi-Wan honored Qui-Gon Jinn's final request and took Anakin as his Padawan learner, and the Sith were exposed.

But a question remained: If Darth Maul was a Sith Lord, was he a student or a Master?

Star Wars: Episode II-Attack of the Clones

Ten years after the reemergence of the Sith, Obi-Wan Kenobi, Anakin Skywalker, and the rest of the Jedi Knights struggled to keep order in the galaxy. Several thousand solar systems threatened to leave the Republic as they followed a Separatist movement led by the mysterious Count Dooku, a former Jedi Knight.

Senator Amidala of Naboo, the former queen, returned to the Galactic Senate to petition for the creation of an army of the Republic to aid the struggling Jedi. Unfortunately, not everyone shared in her vision, and she was under the repeated threat of assassination.

After another failed assassination attempt, the Jedi Order assigned Obi-Wan and Anakin, whom she'd not seen in years, as her personal bodyguards. While they were on assignment, Anakin's impetuous nature got the better of him and he used the senator as bait to draw out her assassin. Still, Amidala's would-be assassin would not relent. She struck once again while Amidala was under the watchful eye of the two Jedi, and the duo chased the assassin down. When they caught her, she was killed by a poisoned dart before she could reveal the name of the person who issued her orders.

While Obi-Wan followed the trail of clues back to a bounty hunter named Jango Fett, Anakin was assigned to protect Senator Amidala while in seclusion on Naboo. The trail to Jango Fett led Obi-Wan to the mysterious planet Kamino. There he found a race of cloners with an army of soldiers they claimed was commissioned by the Jedi Master Sifo-Dyas, who had died over ten years prior. Though he was perplexed by the development, Obi-Wan didn't have much time to mull it over, as Jango Fett attacked him unsuccessfully before fleeing the planet.

Meanwhile, Anakin and Amidala grew closer while in seclusion. Though Anakin was haunted by the memory of his mother, his love for Amidala grew every day they spent together. Eventually, Anakin's concerns about his mother overwhelmed him, and he was drawn away from the hideout in Naboo. With Amidala in tow, Anakin set out in search of his mother only to find that she'd been captured by a Tusken Raider hunting party.

In a failed attempt to rescue his mother, Anakin was briefly reunited with her long enough for her to die in his arms. In a fit of rage, he single-handedly destroyed the entire village of Tusken Raiders. Meanwhile, Jango Fett led Obi-Wan to the Trade Federation planet Geonosis. There, lying amidst a large concentration of Federation ships, was a large battle droid factory. Obi-Wan infiltrated the factory to discover Count Dooku and his followers secretly scheming to destroy the Jedi and overthrow the Republic.

Before he was captured, Obi-Wan sent out a call to Anakin and the Jedi Order. However, instead of following the Jedi Order's instructions to protect Amidala on Naboo, Amidala coerced Anakin into searching for Obi-Wan in hopes of rescuing him. When Anakin and Amidala arrived at Geonosis, they, too, were captured by Dooku's troops. Meanwhile, Supreme Chancellor Palpatine issued orders to create a grand army of the Republic, knowing full well that the army was waiting for him on Kamino. When the Jedi arrived on Geonosis to rescue Obi-Wan, they found that not only was he in danger, but so were Anakin and Amidala. The battle on Geonosis was short but fierce. Just as the Jedi's numbers began to dwindle and all hope seemed to fade, Master Yoda arrived with an army of clone troopers.

Upon seeing Jedi Master Mace Windu defeat his loyal soldier Jango Fett, Count Dooku fled. Anakin and Obi-Wan followed Dooku and cornered him in a cave where the two Jedi engaged the traitorous Count in heated battle. Dooku's skills were far superior, and he was able to fell Obi-Wan and sever Anakin's arm. Just as Dooku was about to destroy Anakin once and for all, Yoda arrived and rescued the two fallen Jedi. Foiled by his former master, Dooku fled once again—this time successfully.

Though he got away, Dooku did inadvertently reveal that a mysterious Darth Sidious was somehow controlling the Senate. Anakin and Amidala secretly married, but the damage had been done. Anakin had already taken his first step toward the dark side, the dark side of the Force grew stronger, and the Clone Wars began.

3

The Clone Wars

The Clone Wars spanned about three years and rapidly spread throughout the galaxy after the Battle of Geonosis. Though Count Dooku seemed the public mastermind of the Separatist strategy, he secretly answered to his Sith Master, Darth Sidious. Military actions were led by the cyborg General Grievous, and Dooku had a cadre of specialized underlings, including the bounty hunter Durge and the dark side warrior Asajj Ventress. Early in the war, Dooku's forces mined the hyperspace routes that connected the Core Worlds to the rest of the galaxy, effectively cutting off the Republic from the bulk of its resources and allowing the Separatists relative freedom of movement in the Outer Rim. To match this maneuver, the Jedi entreated the Hutts to share their control of the Outer Rim, allowing the Republic to move their vessels through Hutt-controlled space.

Over the course of the war, public opinion of the Jedi Order waxed and waned. Their early defeats underscored their vulnerability, and their reluctant adoption of the rank of general caused them to be blamed for many of the missteps in the Clone Wars. Still, there emerged champions like Anakin Skywalker and Obi-Wan Kenobi, respectively dubbed the Hero with No Fear and the Negotiator by an approving public. Of course, similar heroes arose on the side of the Separatists....

How to Use This Book

TIP

Like the debris scattered about the many arenas, these Tip boxes are similarly scattered around the pages of this book. Whenever you see one of these boxes, take a moment to stop and meditate on the information contained within, such as how to increase your abilities, improve as a Republic soldier, and enhance your experience overall.

NOTE

Notes are supplementary bits of info that may not enhance your abilities or experience but will provide info on the game or the book. You can live without these, but if you thirst for knowledge, these are just for you.

CAUTION

Always read Caution boxes. While Notes and Tips may make you a better duelist or a notch smarter, Caution boxes will keep you alive. The sole purpose of Caution boxes is to provide you vital warnings of dangers that lie ahead.

ARTIFACT

Scattered across your various missions are several glowing artifacts. Whenever you see these Artifact Location boxes, read them carefully to find a nearby artifact and add it to your collection.

THE CAST

As you traverse the many planets throughout your adventure, you will take control of different Republic warriors. Whether you're battling as one of the powerful Jedi or as a "shiny"—a rookie clone trooper—you'll need to know what you're in for. This chapter details all of the heroes, villains, and scrap metal you'll encounter throughout your journey.

NOTE

Aside from looking and moving slightly different from each other, all Jedi have the same basic moves and attacks. The same goes for all clone troopers. However, each Jedi does have their own strong, favored attack.

Fighters of the Force

Anakin Skywalker

Obi-Wan's former Padawan is now a general and a Jedi Knight. His daring exploits have made him a Republic hero. Hoping to curb his reckless nature, the Jedi Council have given him his own Padawan, Ahsoka Tano.

Obi-Wan Kenobi

A Jedi Knight and legendary hero of the Republic, Obi-Wan was Anakin's former Master. The two are now firm friends, although Anakin's recklessness is a concern for Obi-Wan.

Ahsoka Tano

An eager and feisty Jedi youngling, Ahsoka was assigned to Anakin Skywalker in the hope that having a Padawan would teach Anakin responsibility.

Mace Windu

Mace Windu is one of the most powerful and respected Jedi, second only to Yoda. As a senior member of the Jedi Council, he prefers diplomacy over war; however, his combat prowess is legendary.

Aayla Secura

Like many other Jedi, the Clone Wars has forced Aayla Secura to become a general. The compassionate and talented Jedi Knight is highly respected by the troops she leads.

Plo Koon

Level-headed and always calm, Plo Koon is a respected member of the Jedi Council. It was Plo Koon who discovered the infant Ahsoka and brought her to the Jedi Temple.

Kit Fisto

A renowned Jedi Master and member of the Jedi Council, Kit Fisto is known for his friendly manner and impressive skills in combat.

Yoda

The longest-serving member of the Jedi Council, the 900-year-old diminutive Jedi Master is the most revered and renowned of all Jedi. His mastery of the Force, his lightsaber skills, and his wisdom are legendary.

Luminara Unduli

Luminara is a Jedi Master, general, and trusted adviser to the Jedi Council and Republic Senate. Her keen powers of observation and incredible talent with the lightsaber have served the Republic well.

NOTE

Of the many Jedi warriors, Master Yoda is the only one you can't take into battle. However, his wisdom will see you through many challenges.

5

Send in the Clones

Captain Rex

Captain Rex [CC-7567] is in command of the famed 501st. He serves as Anakin's second-in-command. He is a tough, freethinking soldier who fears nothing his impulsive and daring general throws at him.

Commander Bly

Commander Bly [CC-5052] is the leader of the renown Star Corps troopers assigned to General Aayla Secura. A deadly soldier on the battlefield, Bly has come to hold a great deal of respect for his Jedi general.

Commander Cody

Commander Cody [CC-2224] is a loyal and no-nonsense commander. Cody shares an easy camaraderie with his general, Obi-Wan, and his battlefield exploits and good leadership have earned him the respect of the Jedi and clone alike.

Commander Gree

Commander Gree [CC-1004] is often employed in the field under General Luminara Unduli. Gree's sharp mind and battle prowess make him an ideal second for the renowned Jedi Master.

Commander Ponds

Commander Ponds [CC-6454] is a hardened veteran who was assigned to Mace Windu after the Battle of Geonosis. Ponds has the phrase "some guys have all the luck" written on the back of his helmet.

Private Switch

Private Switch [CP-6824] is a "soft shell"—a clone designated to technical tasks rather than combat. Despite his expertise in technical matters, Switch has surprised his fellow clones and earned their respect with his resourcefulness and bravery.

"Rookie"

Rookie [CT-3899] is a "shiny" on his first assignment. He is eager to join his fellow clones on the field and put his training to the test.

Sergeant Boomer

Sergeant Boomer [CS-2207] is a "tough as they come" veteran soldier with a tendency to wisecrack. After having fought alongside Captain Rex countless times, Boomer has become one of Rex's most trusted soldiers and a good friend.

Sergeant Kano

Sergeant Kano [CS-1004] is a hard-edged veteran of numerous battles. His latest assignment has him "babysitting" a new squad of "shinies" on the newly liberated world of Ryloth.

The Dark Side

Asajj Ventress

Armed with twin lightsabers, Ventress combines combat and Force skills with her hatred for the Jedi. This makes her the ideal assassin and field commander for Count Dooku.

Battle Tips

Asajj Ventress is a speedy lightsaber duelist. With her twin lightsabers, she can attack and defend with blinding speed. In battle, you'll have to contend with each of her bright red blades. Have your partner take on one blade while you deal with the other. Slowly whittle down her health until she seeks refuge, then use the environment to your advantage. Bring her safe haven crumbling down around her.

Count Dooku

After leaving the Jedi Order, Dooku was lured to the dark side by Darth Sidious. As Sith Lord and leader of the Separatist movement, Dooku—aka Darth Tyranus—is the Republic's most cunning and ruthless foe...that they know of.

Battle Tips

Count Dooku is a proud, overconfident fighter. Use this to your advantage. When you face the traitorous Sith Lord, he'll attempt to use his Sith skill—Force Lightning— to overpower you. When he does, absorb his lightning, then redirect it at one of the nearby generators. When the generator charges, it'll overload and blast the Sith with his own electrical charge. Dooku will be so preoccupied with his own agenda, he'll fail to dodge his own reflected attack.

Darth Sidious

Darth Sidious is a mysterious Sith Lord existing behind a veil of darkness and secrecy. Acting as a puppet master behind the Separatist movement and the Clone Wars, he is determined to eliminate the Jedi Order and destroy the Republic.

NOTE

In keeping with his tendency to remain in the shadows, Darth Sidious will not get his hands dirty... yet. You will not have to face him in battle during this adventure.

Bounty Hunters

Cad Bane

Willing to work for the highest bidder, Cad Bane is a ruthless and resourceful bounty hunter from the planet Duros. No job is too sinister so long as the credits are right.

NOTE

Since Cad values credits above all else, he can be on the Republic's side one minute, then shooting at them the next. Though he crosses your path during your adventure, you will not have to fight him directly, and you even get the chance to play as him.

Kul Teska

Kul Teska is a Skakoan rogue scientist and assassin known for his ruthlessness and excessive methods. He is a master of technology with nothing but contempt for Force users. Teska wears a bulky armored suit equipped with a vast array of weapons.

Battle Tips

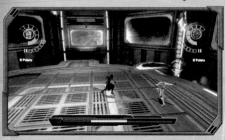

Kul Teska is a stubborn mercenary. He's as tough as they come but rarely changes his tactics, even across several

encounters. In battle, he'll often fight using three basic attacks, all of which you can dodge. His first attack is his grappling hook rush. After whipping out his grappling

hook and grabbing the ground near you, he'll yank himself toward you and rush you like a bull. His second attack is a

flaming cannonball attack in which he speeds toward you and attempts to bowl you over. His final basic assault is his rocket launcher attack. Instead of dodging it, use the Force to bounce his rockets back at him and bring him down to your level. Once he's down, cut through him with lightsaber combos.

NOTE

Depending on the encounter, Teska might also have other secondary attacks. We will show you how to defend against those in the walkthrough when you encounter them.

Lightsaber Fodder

The Separatists put up one heck of a fight. Though they are led by Sith Lords at the highest levels, they use various droids as their tools of war. Whether it's a simple battle droid or a hulking vulture droid, you'll need to know exactly how to handle each type of Separatist droid to make it through your adventure in one piece. After all, you don't want to join the Force prematurely....

Battle Droid

The humanoid-looking but mindless B1 is the mainstay of the Separatist's droid army. Usually equipped with E-5 blaster rifles, B1s can also use jetpacks and fly STAPs.

These clunky soldiers are the weakest link in the Separatist army. Capable of being destroyed with a simple heavy Force Blast or a quick lightsaber combo, the battle droids are usually the first line of defense (or offense) when facing the Separatist forces. In battle, target these clankers early. Though they're weaker and more vulnerable to your attacks, their blasters can still cause a major problem for you during battle. If you see them bunch up or approach in battalion formation, use heavy Force Blasts to demolish them instantly. More often than not, a quick one- to two-hit lightsaber combo will reduce a battle droid to scrap metal, but it's even better to Force Blast, Force Kill, or Lightsaber Throw them, as they normally arrive in groups.

Droid-Jack 101

After double-jumping onto a battle droid's head, you can either execute a jump attack or leap off its head

onto the head of another nearby droid. Because they're generally weak and flimsy, they cannot support a Jedi's weight, making them impossible to droid-jack, commandeer, and then use as a weapon.

Super Battle Droid

The B2 is a bulkier and more powerful improvement on the B1. It is protected by an armored shell and equipped with a built-in blaster in its arm. The B2 also has a grenade variant.

PSP NOTES

The grenade variant of the B2 does not show up in the PSP version of the game.

Super battle droids are larger, tougher, and heavier versions of the battle droids. Though they're still susceptible to lightsaber combos and Force Push attacks, it usually takes several attacks to bring them down. Unlike the battle droids, these super soldiers have stronger, arm-mounted blasters capable of shredding through other droids—or, worse, through you! When facing these droids in battle, either take them down at the same time as other battle droids, or hijack them and use them as weapons against the rest of the enemy battalion.

Droid-Jack 101

More than any other droid, the super battle droid is the best droid to jack. Their arm-mounted blasters are extremely effective against other droids.

Spider Droid

Resembling a mechanical arachnid, these four-legged dome-shaped droids feature a powerful, centrally mounted laser cannon and are capable of climbing vertical surfaces.

Spider droids are small, multilegged droids that act very much like mobile blaster turrets. Capable of crawling up cliff sides, buildings, and other vertical surfaces, spider droids can pop up during a battle when you least expect it. Luckily, they are not reinforced with shielding or other defensive mechanisms. As long as you can avoid its turret blasts, you'll always have a fighting chance to squish these pests.

Droid-Jack 101

After double-jumping atop a spider droid, you can either crush it or jack it. Once it's under your control, the spider droid becomes your own stationary turret, which is capable of blasting super battle droids, obstacles, or other enemies. Though the crawling clankers are surprisingly mobile on their own, they become stationary once you jack them. However, a spider droid's turret can fire in 360 degrees.

TIP

Practice your aiming after droid-jacking a spider droid. The laser sight will help you accurately blast your enemies.

Sabotage Droid

Sabotage droids are black buglike droids equipped with rotor blades, an electrical prod, and laser cannons. Their hovering capability, combined with their rotor blades, make them deadly opponents. Sabotage droids are small, floating droids with mounted laser turrets and cloaking shields. As you traverse the many Separatist-held camps, these droids will often appear and then disappear before your very eyes. Because they are also capable of hovering above the ground, they can often disappear in one area, only to appear above and behind you somewhere else. When that happens, you can try to reach them with jump attacks or jack them to crush them from above. If they attack you with their laser turrets, use evasive movements to stay out of their way until you can double-jump on top of them or Force Blast them.

Droid-Jack 101

If you manage to double-jump onto a sabotage droid, you can jack it and turn it into a devastating kamikaze droid with impressive destructive potential. After jacking it, charge the sabotage droid and aim it at your target. Once its rotors have reached their maximum speed, let the droid fly and blow up your target. One sabotage droid can take out medium-sized groups of battle droids, several super battle droids, other sabotage droids, and obstacles!

9

Chameleon Droid

The chameleon droid is a stealthy mine-laying droid capable of making itself invisible by projecting surrounding imagery onto itself. This droid is armed with laser cannons and can climb vertical surfaces.

Chameleon droids, not to be confused with other cloaking-capable droids or spider droids, are small, multilegged droids that lay troublesome mines in your way. Like the sabotage droid, chameleon droids can disappear and reappear at will and can often scurry about with surprising speed. Though these little guys aren't quite as dangerous as other blaster-toting droids, their mines can cause major damage if you're not careful. To make short work of these bothersome clankers, use jump attacks and Force Blasts.

Droid-Jack 101

Droid-jack a chameleon droid when you need mines to destroy an obstacle or to lay mines around an area and intercept other attacking droids.

Droideka (Destroyer Droid)

The destroyer droid is a powerful droid equipped with a pair of twin blasters, a protective energy shield, and the ability to transform into a wheel-like configuration that can roll at high speed.

By far the most dangerous of all the droids, these rolling death balls are both hard to defend against and difficult to take out. The only shielded droid, the droideka also has extremely powerful turrets that can fire off powerful, nearly endless streams of blaster fire! When fighting as a Jedi, either Force Push it into a wall with a heavy Force Blast, then jack it, or rush it while its shields are down. If you're fighting it as a clone trooper, use your secondary weapons to disrupt its shield, then blast it to bits. Better yet, catch these droids with a jump attack while they're rolling into place.

CAUTION

Act quickly after disrupting a droideka's shields. If you wait too long, they'll regenerate their shields and resume their firing.

Droid-Jack 101

After knocking off a droideka's shields, you can jack it and turn it into a droid bowling ball. Charge the droideka, then let it loose on the other nearby droids to knock them over or blow them up. But be careful: the droideka will bounce back and forth when it hits an obstacle, so stay out of its way if it bounces back in your direction! Alternatively, you can roll it around by jumping onto it and not jacking it.

Crab Droid

These huge bronze-colored crablike droids can scale vertical surfaces. Crab droids are equipped with heavily armored legs capable of generating a deadly shock wave and dealing heavy damage in close melee combat.

These large brutes can stand up on their rear two claws and come down with their front two claws, creating a shock wave of energy. Standard lightsaber combos can be effective against them, but only when attacking from the side; otherwise you risk standing in the path of its shock-wave attack. These droids can block both in front and behind them, so hit them from one side and then jump onto them, or move around them and hit the unguarded side.

Droid-Jack 101

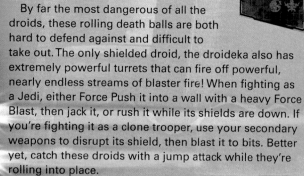

Use the crab droid to unleash crushing shock-wave attacks on large groups of droids and even take them out from a distance. Charge the attack as it rears, then smash it down for better results. When it comes to droid-jacking large clankers, it gets no better than this.

Magna Guards

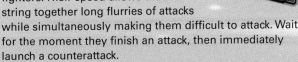

Aside from battle droids and super battle droids, magna guards are the only other humanoid droids you'll encounter. These tough clankers possess almost Jedi-like speed and agility, and their electro-staffs make them highly adept weapon fighters. Their speed allows them to string together long flurries of attacks while simultaneously making them difficult to attack. Wait for the moment they finish an attack, then immediately launch a counterattack.

Droid-Jack 101

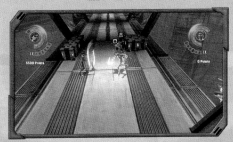

Magna guards are capable of being droid-jacked, but not quite as easily as other droids. They can repel your attempts to droid-jack them except while they're blocking. Once you've tapped into a magna guard's control servos, you can maneuver the guard around the battlefield using its electro-staff to clear a path through other droids. You can also use the magna guards against other magna guards in sticky situations!

Vulture Droid

Vulture droids are large, imposing clankers with a ton of firepower. Normally, these droids stand in one place and don't move much, so it's up to you to remain mobile and evasive. Dodge its attacks and wait for your partner to lock down on one of its oversized legs, then rush its stuck leg and slice it with your lightsaber. You can also use the Force to grab the droid's legs yourself. Once the vulture droid drops, rush onto its head and ram your lightsaber into its chrome dome.

PSP NOTES

There are no vulture droids on Jedi levels on the PSP.

Octuptarra Droid

Of the many droids you will encounter, the octuptarra droid is by far the largest. These huge clankers stomp around the battlefield while their three blaster turrets try to pepper you with fire until you're one with the Force. To confront this droid, you or your partner should lock down on one of its legs using the Force. Once in place, climb up the leg, then double-jump onto one of the turrets and slice it off. Do this two times to slice off two of its turrets, then use the third as a launcher to get atop the head and bring the huge beast down!

NOTE

The vulture and octuptarra droids cannot be droid-jacked!

THE WAYS OF THE FORCE

Heads-up Display

1. **Player:** This is the picture of the Republic soldier you currently command.

2. **Health bar:** As you take damage, this Health bar slowly depletes. When it is all gone, you'll have only a few more hits before you become one with the Force.

3. **Combo meter:** As you attack enemies in quick succession, this slowly fills up in three stages. The more it fills up, the more points you will accrue from defeating Separatist scum.

PSP AND WII NOTES

On the Wii, the Combo meter fills up to 5 stages. On the PSP, it fills up to 10 stages.

4. **Force points:** This keeps track of your current Force points. Increase this number by acquiring point spheres, shattering point crystals, or defeating enemies. Force points can be used to purchase upgrades, cheats, and other nifty unlockables.

5. **Power-up indicator:** The shield surrounding your player icon changes color and form depending on the current power-up you picked up. Power-ups grant you different abilities, depending on what color they are:

Power-up	Color	Effect
Damage*	Red	Deals double damage
Invincibility*	White	Player becomes temporarily invincible
Combo*	Yellow	Combo bar will fill and will not cool down temporarily
Force Multiplier*	Blue	Point multiplier doubles
Force Blast*	Cyan	Force Push automatically becomes Force Blast

* All power-ups last 15 seconds.

TIP

We strongly recommend you read the manual for your version of *Star Wars: The Clone Wars—Republic Heroes*. Basic actions like running and jumping are covered in the manual. And while some of the information below is also covered by Master Yoda during your adventure, we've included it below for quick reference.

Adventuring

To many would-be Republic soldiers, adventuring across foreign planets is second nature. But if you don't know how to navigate treacherous terrain, then you could find yourself plummeting to your demise or accidentally missing a necessary ledge. The following pages cover all the necessary skills to get you safely from point A to point B. Practice all of the following skills to keep them sharp and keep you alive.

NOTE

A Jedi's high midi-chlorian count improves his reflexes beyond natural standards. Because Jedi possess increased agility, speed, and strength, they can do things that the clone soldiers cannot. The abilities available to Jedi are different from those available to the clones.

Sliding

Console	Command
Xbox 360	Run toward target or obstacle, then press ⓑ
PS3/PS2	Run toward target or obstacle, then press ■
Wii	Run toward target or obstacle, then press ②
PSP	Run toward target or obstacle, then press the left trigger

A Jedi can slide underneath low barriers and even droids! Though this ability is context sensitive while adventuring, you can always execute slide attacks on short, crawling clankers like spider droids or chameleon droids.

Double-Jumps

Console	Command
Xbox 360	Press ⓐ, ⓐ
PS3/PS2	Press ✕, ✕
Wii	Press ②, ②
PSP	Press ⇩, ⇩

The double-jump is an extremely useful technique both in and out of combat. Use it to reach distant ledges, to hop atop droids, or to begin jump attacks. However, you must always be careful when double-jumping. If you mistime the second jump while you're in the air, you may launch yourself farther than expected and either go over a ledge or land directly in the center of a hostile droid battalion rather than atop an enemy!

Evasive Backflips

Console	Command
Xbox 360	Hold ⓛⓣ, then press ⓐ
PS3/PS2	Hold ⓛ②, then press ✕

PSP AND WII NOTES

This move is not available in the Wii or PSP versions of the game.

With the Jedi's superior speed and agility, it is typically difficult to hit them with blaster fire or melee attacks. However, once a Jedi begins to engage in evasive maneuvers like backflips, it's nearly impossible to touch them! Use this evasive technique to dodge boss attacks like laser beams, cannonball attacks, and even blaster fire.

Lightsaber Sliding

Console	Command
Xbox 360	Jump toward wall
PS3/PS2	Jump toward wall
Wii	Jump toward wall
PSP	—

The lightsaber sliding technique is actually easy to execute and extremely useful in multileveled areas. Rather than drop down into a potentially dangerous situation, use the lightsaber slide to safely slide down the length of a long shaft to its bottom. After leaping out toward a wall, you'll stab it with your lightsaber and slowly slide down.

13

Wall-Bounding

Console	Command
Xbox 360	Press Ⓐ toward wall, then Ⓐ again as you hit the wall
PS3/PS2	Press ✕ toward wall, then ✕ again as you hit the wall
Wii	Press ② toward wall, then ② again as you hit the wall
PSP	—

Navigating Ledges

Console	Command
Xbox 360	Jump toward or creep out onto ledge, then use Ⓡ to run along ledge while holding the ledge
PS3/PS2	Jump toward or creep out onto ledge, then use right (ANALOG) to run along ledge while holding it
Wii	Jump toward or creep out onto ledge, use Ⓒ to run along ledge while holding it
PSP	—

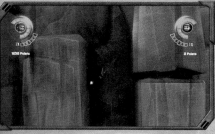

Some areas can be very hard to reach. In fact, the only way to safely reach a high ledge or upper level is to jump back and forth between two nearby walls. The key to wall-bounding is to angle the analog stick toward your destination before jumping. You can also use this technique to safely reach lower levels by jumping back and forth between walls, as you lightsaber slide down the walls of a shaft.

Some areas will be well out of your reach, even with a double-jump. In those cases, you must rely on your ability to navigate perilous ledges. To reach them, jump toward your desired area. If you can reach the area's edge, you'll automatically grab on to it with both hands. If the ledge is long or reaches around to a new area (which happens often), you can run along the edge as you hold on to it with one hand.

Pick-ups and Mission Ranks

Checkpoint Markers

Scattered throughout your adventures are several small glowing checkpoint markers. As you step over one, it'll light up, indicating you've reached a checkpoint. These checkpoints serve as mission trackers, reminding you that you've reached a new area, and they serve as restart markers if you are defeated. When defeated, you'll lose points and reemerge at the nearest checkpoint marker. Similarly, if you get too far ahead of your companion, you'll automatically warp your partner to the nearest checkpoint marker. Note that this does not apply to Co-op mode.

Point Spheres

Like checkpoints, point spheres are scattered all over each mission. These glowing blue orbs are worth 10 Force points each. At times they'll sprawl out ahead of you like a trail of bread crumbs, lighting the path ahead of you. You can also extract them from enemies during combat or find them hidden inside point crystals. Collect as many of these as you can during your adventures to gain a better rank at the end of each mission.

14

Point Crystals

Like point spheres, these crystals are large glowing objects that are littered all throughout your missions. Break them to gain 100 Force points!

Mission Ranks

At the end of each mission, you're graded on your performance. Depending on how

many Force points you collect, you'll get a Bronze, Silver, Gold, or Platinum mission rank. The required amount for each rank depends on the mission completed, so try to get as many Force points as possible during each mission. The Force points you gather during mission challenges also go toward your mission rank.

There are several ways to increase your Force points throughout a mission:

- Collect point spheres
- Shatter point crystals
- Complete mission challenges
- Destroy enemies

 TIP

Increase your point multiplier with combos or power-ups.

 TIP

For mission rank requirements for every mission, see the Mission Rank table in the "Mission Challenges" chapter.

15

Mission Challenges

Mission challenges are short 30- to 180-second trials that appear throughout your missions.

At times, they will appear automatically as you progress through the level, while sometimes they require that you defeat all of the enemies in a certain area. There are four types of mission challenges:

- **Droid Demolition:** Defeat as many droids as possible any way you choose within the given time limit.
- **Point Panic:** Pick up as many point spheres as possible within the time limit.
- **Knockback Knockout:** Use the Force to push droids off ledges or into hazards.
- **Takeover Takedown:** Destroy droids by using only other droids.

These short mission challenges are lucrative ways to increase your Force points to get better mission rank or to unlock a new upgrade or cheat. Because each challenge will be different depending on the location at which

it takes place and the person playing with you (or the computer), we can't give you specific strategy for each mission challenge. Instead, we'll provide you general tips you can use for each of the four challenge types.

Droid Demolition Tips

Since Droid Demolition challenges are no-holds-barred competitions in which you must maul and mangle the most clankers, there's no real set of rules for this challenge type. You can, however, maximize the amount of droids you demolish by varying your techniques and knowing which droids to destroy first. Always target the battle droids first during these challenges. They're easier to destroy and usually appear in larger quantities than other droids. If a super battle droid appears nearby, jack it and use it as a weapon to bulldoze the other droids.

If you keep the fight on the ground, be sure to vary your lightsaber combos. Also note that if your partner has weakened a droid and you finish it off with a simple Force Blast, you'll get the points for destroying it!

Point Panic Tips

Your biggest enemy during a Point Panic challenge is yourself! Since there are no enemies to fend off, all you need to do is collect the point spheres before the time runs out. Unfortunately, the terrain usually provides a challenge as well. The best strategy for tackling any Point Panic challenge is to find an easy route along the point-riddled path and follow it closely to a large pool of points. Since the point spheres regenerate after you collect them, you can usually turn around and follow the path back or simply cycle back around to the beginning of the path and collect more points.

Don't take any unnecessary risks while collecting points. If you fall off a narrow ledge or fail to catch a nearby beam, you'll fall to your death and waste precious time while you regenerate at the checkpoint. In that time, your opponent, who may have been more careful, could be easily grabbing more point spheres and taking the lead. Remember that all sources of points count toward Point Panic challenges, and killing droids gets you more points than Force orbs. Use the Combo meter cheat and increase your Combo meter to maximize your final score.

PSP NOTES

Point Panic challenges are not available in the PSP version of the game.

Knockback Knockout Tips

These challenges always take place on ledges, cliff sides, or platforms. The trick here is to not waste too much time knocking enemies over the side. The quicker you knock them over, the more you'll be able to Force Push over the edge. As always, concentrate on the weaker, lighter battle droids first. Use heavy Force Blasts to send them flying.

Super battle droids also make good targets during these challenges. Finish them off with heavy Force Blasts to knock them over permanently. Always keep in mind the droid's starting location so you can anticipate where they will approach from first.

PSP NOTES

Knockback Knockout challenges are not available in the PSP version of the game.

Takeover Takedown Tips

Takeover Takedown challenges are fast and fun. During these challenges, you acquire points only by eliminating droids while droid-jacking a more powerful droid; therefore, target the most powerful droid first and jack it! Super battle droids and crab droids are among the most effective to use in the challenges. Super battle droids can shred through large groups of droids, while the crab droid's shock-wave attack can destroy several clankers at once.

If push comes to shove, droid-jack a spider droid. Their laser-sight targeting helps you lay waste to your enemies. While a sabotage droid can wipe out several clankers at once, their charge requirement wastes too much time and allows your competition to clean the area before you can even let the sabotage droid loose.

Advanced Combat

It is often said that the Jedi, his lightsaber, and the Force are all intertwined. They are one. Therefore, a Jedi's fighting technique always combines all three to create one fluid, nearly unstoppable weapon. If a Jedi is not attacking with his blade, then he is using the Force. If he is not attacking with the Force, then he is using his keen intellect and Jedi wisdom to formulate a plan of attack. If he is not formulating a plan of attack, then he is letting his lightsaber dance with the enemy. At any given point in battle, the Jedi, his lightsaber, and the Force are always at work.

The following advanced combat techniques assume you're mastered the ability to string together simple lightsaber combos and use the Force to blast enemies from a distance. With the basics in mind, build upon your arsenal to become the most powerful Jedi possible.

NOTE
We have excluded clone troopers from the "Advanced Combat" section, because they cannot execute combos, use the Force, or droid-jack enemies.

Combination Attacks

After mastering simple multistrike combos with the lightsaber, you're ready to add multiple forms of attack to your technique. By combining lightsaber strikes with Force blows, you can effectively destroy large amounts of enemy droids in one long, fluid stream of attacks. Combination attacks are also used to increase your Combo meter to gain more points. Always open with at least one lightsaber attack of droid-hop for this purpose, and then do everything possible to avoid getting hit, as it will reset your Combo bar.

Generally speaking, large-sweeping and area attacks are best used early. This will kill all the battle droids in one hit and will weaken the others. Use lightsaber attacks to take out the small, singular droids, as they will deflect fire and stun other droids with generally quicker animations, leaving you less vulnerable. Don't let your enemy get behind you when using lightsaber attacks, as you will *not* deflect fire. Time your strikes carefully to make sure you attack all of your enemies equally. Continue shifting your attacks between all surrounding enemies until only three or four are left; then double-jump atop one of them and either jack it or use a jump attack to crush the remaining droids.

17

Using the Force

It is often easy to neglect the Force and rely solely on your lightsaber skills. While not all Force attacks are necessarily *destructive*, such as the Force Push, the Force is often the only weapon you will need to eliminate enemies. Heavy Force Blast attacks can shove enemies off ledges, bridges, and other precarious platforms. Once they're near the edge, hit them with a heavy Force Blast to send them flying. Use Force Push to shove enemies into each other, over ledges, and into hazards; you can even do this with many enemies at a time!

Perhaps the best use of the Force is to bounce enemy rockets back at them across chasms or to fling objects at your targets. While this may not inflict damage on the enemy, it will stun them. While they are stunned, use your time wisely. Either rush the stunned enemies as you reflect blaster fire at the other droids in the group, or leap into their midst and crush the stunned droids and their soldier buddies. Of course, you can also droid-jack the stunned droid, wreaking havoc in the process. Use these two techniques when engaged in combat to create breathing room from approaching enemies or to destroy weaker enemies like battle droids.

Droid-Jacking

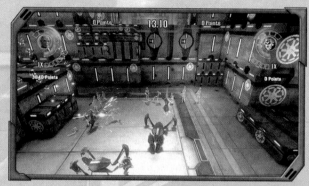

Droid-jacking is an integral part of combat. Every droid—except battle, vulture, and octuptarra droids—can be jacked and used against other droids. To do so, double-jump onto the target droid and ram your lightsaber into it to take control. Once you've jacked the droid, you can direct it around the battlefield (with the exception of the crab droid and sabotage droid) and use its weapons systems to attack!

You can force sabotage droids to self-destruct and take out obstacles, larger enemies, or lay mines!

TIP

For information on what droids can do after you jack them, see the "Droid-Jack 101" sections in "The Cast" chapter.

Vehicles

At times, you'll often be required to ride on vehicles to complete your mission. Whether it's speeding down a long tunnel on a STAP or riding a hulking AT-RT walker across an explosive battlefield, you'll need to know what is what in order to stay safe and complete your mission successfully.

AT-RT Walkers

Designed primarily as a reconnaissance vehicle, the rugged AT-RT (All Terrain Recon Transport) is also armed with a blaster cannon. This allows a single clone to become a powerful anti-infantry unit.

These tall, two-legged, manned walkers are the perfect patrol vehicles for clone troopers. With a high-powered mounted cannon and strong leaping abilities, the AT-RT is a highly mobile, destructive force. The only downside is that they're rather slow to maneuver and often leave you open to return fire. While using one of these tall transports, be mindful of the areas you walk into. Don't storm ahead blindly or rush around corners, because you might find yourself surrounded instantly.

AT-TE Walkers

The AT-TE (All Terrain Tactical Enforcer) is a powerful six-legged armored assault vehicle, armed with four turret lasers at the front and a heavy cannon turret mounted atop the vehicle.

Though you won't ever pilot one, you'll often ride on the back or front of an AT-TE walker as it tramples across a battlefield. The large platform on the AT-TE's back is perfect for holding impromptu battles or riding safely through blaster fire below you. Because these powerful vehicles can traipse up the side of a cliff, the vehicle's tips are equipped with a small platform capable of supporting two or three soldiers.

STAP

STAPs (single trooper aerial platforms) are lightweight reconnaissance vehicles, armed with laser cannons and capable of low-altitude flight. They're designed to be used by battle droids. Though quick, STAPs leave the rider exposed to enemy fire.

STAPs are actually Separatist vehicles manned by battle droids during combat. Like the AT-RT, these are equipped with moderately powered blasters with an impressive rate of fire. What they lack in destructive power they make up for in speed and agility. Capable of turning on a dime, these vehicles are often used as escape vehicles. Use Force Blasts or double-jump onto them to remove their battle droids and claim them for yourself.

LAAT

The LAAT (Low Altitude Assault Transport) is a hardy multiweapon gunship that can serve as an air-to-air and air-to-ground support vehicle as well as a troop transport for clone troops.

NOTE

The LAAT serves only as a transport vehicle. As such, you will not pilot them or ride them during a mission.

ACT 1

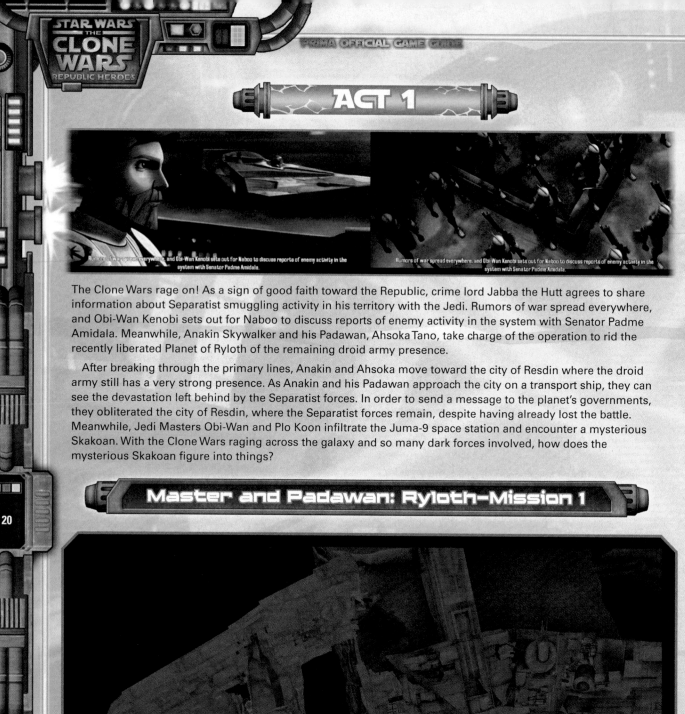

Rumors of war spread everywhere, and Obi-Wan Kenobi sets out for Naboo to discuss reports of enemy activity in the system with Senator Padme Amidala.

Rumors of war spread everywhere, and Obi-Wan Kenobi sets out for Naboo to discuss reports of enemy activity in the system with Senator Padme Amidala.

The Clone Wars rage on! As a sign of good faith toward the Republic, crime lord Jabba the Hutt agrees to share information about Separatist smuggling activity in his territory with the Jedi. Rumors of war spread everywhere, and Obi-Wan Kenobi sets out for Naboo to discuss reports of enemy activity in the system with Senator Padme Amidala. Meanwhile, Anakin Skywalker and his Padawan, Ahsoka Tano, take charge of the operation to rid the recently liberated Planet of Ryloth of the remaining droid army presence.

After breaking through the primary lines, Anakin and Ahsoka move toward the city of Resdin where the droid army still has a very strong presence. As Anakin and his Padawan approach the city on a transport ship, they can see the devastation left behind by the Separatist forces. In order to send a message to the planet's governments, they obliterated the city of Resdin, where the Separatist forces remain, despite having already lost the battle. Meanwhile, Jedi Masters Obi-Wan and Plo Koon infiltrate the Juma-9 space station and encounter a mysterious Skakoan. With the Clone Wars raging across the galaxy and so many dark forces involved, how does the mysterious Skakoan figure into things?

Master and Padawan: Ryloth-Mission 1

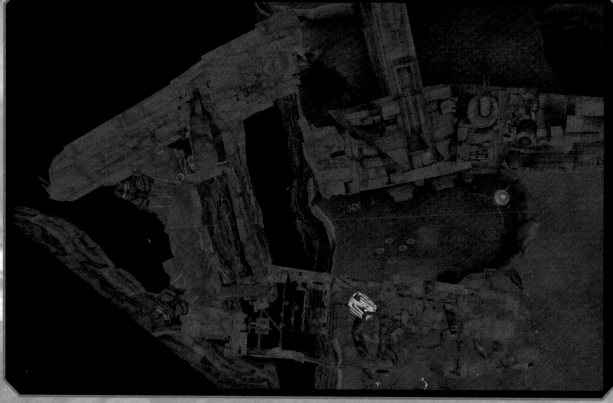

As the Clone Wars rage on across the galaxy, small planets are engulfed in the turmoil. The Separatists don't care whether a planet can sustain a full-out battle, while the Republic desperately tries to quell the evil Rebellion wherever it arises. On the planet of Ryloth, clone troopers rush the battlefield as the Separatists' battle droids unleash a devastating wave of blaster fire.

When the clone troopers hit the battle droids' wall of blaster fire, they immediately rush for cover. As they do, Anakin Skywalker and Ahsoka Tano bring up the rear, lightsabers swinging in a dazzling display of sword mastery. Their lightsabers cut through the battle droids like a hot blade through butter, but they, too, hit the wall of battle droid blaster fire.

Since the path ahead is heavily guarded by Separatist forces, Anakin Skywalker deftly leaps and bounds atop a nearby precipice with his Padawan in tow. If they can't go through the enemy army, they'll go above it!

NOTE

Once Anakin and Ahsoka have climbed up the nearby cliff side, you gain control of Anakin.

Go Around, You Must, if You Cannot Go Through...

As Anakin, jump left atop the destroyed bridge. The path ahead is in ruins, but your Jedi agility will allow you to deftly maneuver across small ledges, over precarious drops, and past dangerous platforms. Jump across the next gap, activating your first checkpoint, then creep up to the ledge of the broken bridge and onto the small twisted pipe ahead. Follow the pipe to its end, then double-jump across the pipe either to the right (to the small L-shaped walkway) or straight ahead to the next pipe section.

TIP

You are your own master while adventuring across a foreign planet's terrain. You'll often be forced to choose one path or another, depending on the situation. Luckily, both paths always lead to the same destination, making the choice of path a matter of taste. No matter the choice, always tread carefully, as you never know what may lie ahead.

Both paths lead to a small barrel-shaped object hanging nearby. Double-jump onto it, then bound to the right, onto another long tube. This tube leads to a second barrel-shaped object hanging between you and the next long platform.

21

STAR WARS
THE
CLONE
WARS
REPUBLIC HEROES

PRIMA OFFICIAL GAME GUIDE

Double-jump onto the long platform and edge toward the series of barrel objects in front of you. Leap from barrel to barrel until you are on the small, square platform. Finally, leap across the small gap

ahead, onto a large stable walkway.

Just as you hit the long walkway, the supports underneath give way and the platform falls, coming to rest at an angle. Safely slide down the fallen walkway and approach the small pile of crates blocking your path.

Do as Master Yoda says and use the Force to blast through the pile of crates. As the crates go crumbling down the

cliff side, they expose a very thin walkway leading across a long gap.

Creep across the gap until you reach the next checkpoint. There, Master Yoda will point out another stack

of crates, guarded by a battle droid perched on a distant pillar. You can't reach the pillar with a double-jump, so charge a Force Blast and let it loose across the large chasm.

When the blast hits the crates, they smash into the battle droid, ridding the pillar of your enemy. Continue

to the end of the cliff, where you'll come across a small battle droid troop in the area below.

Pounce on the battle droids below and let your lightsaber fly. As the battle droids scramble about, double-jump atop their heads and droid-jack them to make quick and easy work of them. If you have a hard time landing directly over their heads, a few short lightsaber strikes should do the trick.

After taking out the first troop of battle droids, a second wave comes marching out from the left and the right. Let Snips (Anakin's nickname for Ahsoka) handle one side while you run your lightsaber through the

battle droids on the other side. Slice through the next few waves of battle droids until the super battle droids come storming out to join the fight.

When they do, follow Master Yoda's instructions and hijack a super battle droid. While in control, guide your droid puppet and aim its blasters at the pillars on the right. Obliterate the two pillars, then hop off your droid and help Ahsoka smash the rest of them.

Leap across the pillars onto the next small cliff. As you land on the cliff, two battle droids swoop by on STAP

vehicles and take position over the next large chasm.

Sneak up behind them and double-jump onto one of the STAPs. Hijack the vehicle and speed across the chasm. On the other side of the gap, dismount the STAP and use the rubble on the area's far wall to climb

up onto the cliff on the right.

then hop off and use a Force Blast to slam some of the nearby debris into the next wave of troops.

Just past the enemy encampment is an octuptarra droid, equipped with three blaster turrets! It stomps around the circular courtyard as it tries to squash you underneath its metal feet. Sprint

away from the robot's feet and wait for one of them to get stuck in the dirt. When it does, turn around and hit it with a series of Force Blasts to hold it in place.

Once the clanker's foot is locked in the dirt, climb atop the long spindly leg and approach the body. Double-jump from the leg onto the droid's blaster turret and hit it with a few lightsaber strikes. You chop off the turret just as the leg comes loose, so hop back down and start scurrying around again.

Walk up to the cliff's edge and locate the next droid troop below. This time, there are two super battle droids with a small complement of regular battle droids stationed nearby. Either use a super-jump attack or drop down onto the super battle droids and droid-jack one of them. Use it to blast through the weaker battle droids,

After destroying the first turret, stay in the same general area. Don't sprint too far from the droid's feet or it'll take longer for one of the feet to get stuck. Instead, let it stomp away at the ground while you dodge the turret blaster fire until it gets stuck again. Repeat this process to destroy the second turret, then use the third turret to launch yourself onto the top of the octuptarra and take it down!

With the turrets disabled, the clanker is no longer capable of operating. It falls to the ground like a sack of protocol droid parts, sending a cloud of dust into the air. As the dust settles, Captain Rex reaches you and your

The Scouts report that's the last of the clankers in this sector.

Padawan. He reports that your overgrown spider droid was the last of the clankers in the general vicinity.

Unfortunately, there are still large pockets of resistance in the city, so you and Captain Rex are not finished yet.

Powering up Resdin: Ryloth—Mission 2

Artifact #1

Artifact PSP #1

The transport vessel touches down in the city, and the Republic troops fan out. Unfortunately, the power to the holo-bridges is in the outer sectors. If the clone troops are going to press into the city, they'll need the bridges. Your task is clear: bring the holo-bridges back online for your troops!

The Separatist fleet may have left the system, but the Droid Army still has a strong presence in Resdin.

Support His Troops, a Jedi Must...

The Separatists may have lost the battle, but they're still dug in deep around the city. Set out on your hunt for the generators! Lead your Padawan right, around the large multilegged transport vehicles.

In the background is a wall with a gap in it, lined with point spheres. Pass it by and continue to the right, past another large transport vehicle. There you'll find a small group of clone troops gathered around a glowing object—an artifact. Grab the artifact, then turn back around and return to the gap in the wall.

ARTIFACT

An artifact is located at the far edge of the starting area. Pass all of the multilegged transport vehicles and find it surrounded by several clone troopers.

PSP AND WII NOTES

In the Wii and PSP versions, you won't see these clone troopers. Also, the artifact is located on a ledge to the right of the generator, which you can find after crossing a crashed LAAT.

NOTE

This is the first of many artifacts! Collect these for some very special rewards:

PS3 and Xbox 360: Unlock special cheats, characters, and more

Wii: Unlock special items in the databank

PSP: Earn 1,000 Player Points!

Step into the gap in the wall and face one side. Leap forward, then angle the analog stick toward the opposite wall and jump toward it. Bound back and forth between walls, going higher and grabbing the point spheres as you climb the gap. When you reach the top, grab on to the ledge and hoist yourself up.

From the right side of the gap, edge close to the ledge and hang down from it with one hand. Run along the wall, hanging from one hand, and round the half-circular building, grabbing more point spheres as you go. When you reach the end, hoist yourself back up onto the ledge and destroy the point crystal nearby.

Walk down the ledge and cross the cracked bridge. At its end is a large, almost destroyed cylindrical building with several more point spheres.

PSP NOTES

The building you run on will be straight in the PSP version.

Double-jump from the bridge to the broken half-circle nearby. Carefully creep along the half-circle to its end, then hop down onto the next ledge along the far wall. Follow it up to the gap in the ledge, then hop across. Jump onto the small platform ahead of you, turn around, then hop back onto the next ledge behind you.

25

As you cross the final ledge, you spy a small droid battalion ahead. They're on their guard and on the lookout for Jedi infiltrators. Reach the end of the ledge and bust the next point crystal.

There's no point in waiting—take the fight to the droids! Hop on the small decline and slide down into the thick of things.

As you descend, let Ahsoka take the troops on the left while you dash toward the gold super battle droid on the far right. Hop atop its head and droid-jack it. Ride the robot around the area while you blast its rickety friends apart!

Once you've reduced the first droid wave to a pile of junk parts, a second wave of battle droids swoops in on jetpacks. As they arrive, several more super battle droids appear from the small doorway on the far wall. Greet the battle droids with a Force Blast and send some of them flying off the ledge.

Once the battle droids are no more, turn around and help Ahsoka with the super battle droids. Either smash them from above or droid-jack one of them to turn it on its cohorts. Fend off the next two waves of battle droids and the area is yours.

With the area clear, turn toward the glowing generator along the left wall. Hit it with Force Blasts until it comes back online. When it does, the large circular platform to your right comes to life, slowly rising and falling back down again. Hop atop the platform and ride it up to the next level.

Leap across the small gap between buildings and turn right. Jump from ledge to ledge, moving right as you go and grabbing all the point spheres along the way. Follow the point spheres up to the thin ledge jutting out of the nearby building, then creep left.

Hop onto the large structure below, then edge up to its other side. When you approach the end, a

sabotage droid appears ahead of you. It deactivates its cloaking device, revealing itself for only a few seconds.

When the floating sabotage droid appears, double-jump onto it but do not droid-jack it. Instead,

use it as you would a platform: leap off of it onto the small balcony on the other side. Enter the archway on the balcony and dash across the small building to the other side.

Hop from your balcony to the thin pillar below, then spring from pillar to precarious pillar until you reach the top of the next small building.

At the building's end is a long pole sticking out of its side. Do as Master Yoda says and leap to the pole,

grabbing it while it midair. Swing from the pole onto the next area and land safely on solid ground. Walk to the area's end and find a tall gap in the far left corner.

Step into the gap and bounce up as you did before, grabbing all of the point spheres as you go. When you reach the top, hop to the area below and destroy the battle droids camped out nearby.

Sneak to the building's edge and jump out to the nearest pole. Swing from it to the next one, and then again to the third pole nearby. When you grab ahold of the third pole, stop and turn around to face the way you came.

Swing back across the chasm, up to the next ledge. From here, you can see the second generator tucked away high in a distant corner. Either climb up to the deactivated circular platform or near to the

ledge you used to hoist yourself up. From the platform, you can double-jump onto a long, thin plank that hugs the wall and goes around the generator's corner. The second path leads to the opposite end of the thin plank, but you'll need to jump across two floating droids to reach it.

Reach the generator and hit it with several Force Blasts to bring it back online. Activate the generator and the platform turns on. Backtrack to the circular platform and ride up to the next area.

When you reach the top, several battle droids greet you. Slash through them and a floating sabotage

droid appears nearby. Double-jump onto the sabotage droid and droid-jack it. Wind up the droid, aim it at the doorway with the debris blocking it, and let the droid fly into it, blasting it open.

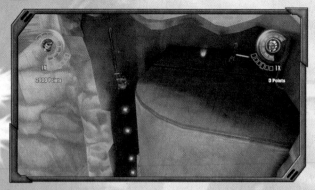

Proceed through the doorway and use a lightsaber slide to drop down the wall on the end. When you land, another droid battalion ambushes you. Droid-jack the nearest super battle droid and turn it on the rest of the company. Clear the first small battalion and a second wave appears, this time with sabotage droids!

Just give us the word and they're scrap metal, General.

PSP NOTES

In the PSP version, a super battle droid will not appear in this location.

With the generators back online, the holo-bridges activate, allowing the Republic forces to march into the city. Though the mission was a success, it is only the first step in liberating Resdin. As soon as your forces enter the city, they find a company of clankers dug in deep. Luckily, your men are up to the task and volunteer to take them out!

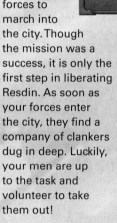

Then the sabotage droids appear, double-jump onto one of them and send it crashing into the next wave of droids. Destroy the final wave, then activate the final generator along the far right wall.

TIP

For tips on how to beat the Droid Demolition mission challenge that appears, see the "Droid Demolition Tips" section in the Ways of the Force chapter.

Outpost Initiation: Ryloth-Mission 3

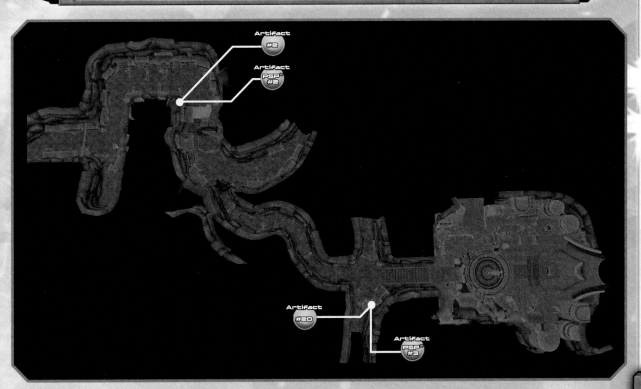

Artifact
#2

Artifact
PSP
#2

Artifact
#20

Artifact
PSP
#3

Though the city is still under siege, the Republic forces have broken through with the aid of the Jedi Knights. Upon finding pockets of Separatist droids around the city, the clone troops volunteer to sweep the area clean of all enemies. Their task is to neutralize the nearest outpost.

NOTE

During this mission, you play as a rookie, Sergeant Kano.

Strength in Numbers, There Is

Lead your four-man squad into the city. Open fire on the battle droids down the street. Turn left up the street and get behind your men. Blast the droids down the street, then rush out from behind your men and advance your forces.

Make a right, then take cover behind the small stone walls. Open fire on the enemy forces ahead and wait for a lull in the firefight. When the firefight dies down for a moment, rush out from behind your cover and sprint to the small wall farther up the street.

29

TIP

If you're feeling dangerous, you can also approach this area by simply strafing left and right, shooting down the droids. It'll be faster and get you more points!

From your new cover, ambush the next few waves of battle droids. Chuck several electro-grenades into the waves of oncoming droids and stun them before they can cause any damage. Destroy the droids while they're stunned.

TIP

When playing as a clone trooper, remember that you're part of a team. Work with each other as a master and Padawan would.

Turn right and take out the gold battle droid perched atop the ledge. Move forward after destroying the droid and take the fight into the courtyard ahead. There, a super battle droid bursts out of a room on the far end of the courtyard, exposing an explosive-grenade reload station.

PSP NOTES

No gold battle droid is present in the PSP version.

ARTIFACT

An artifact is hiding inside a small, dilapidated room on the courtyard's right side. Grab it while you're seeking cover from enemy fire.

Stun the super battle droid with an electro-grenade, then rush past it to grab some explosive grenades. Sprint back out of the small room and toss an explosive grenade at the super battle droids holding position on

the roof of the building at the courtyard's far end.

When the grenade detonates, it takes out the super battle droids and collapses the roof on the battle droids below. Two birds, one stone!

Restock on explosive grenades before leaving the area.

TIP

Alternatively, you can shoot the super battle droid that emerges from behind the building that contains the artifact, and then rush to the grenade-drop location while firing at the remaining droids.

them up, allowing you to finish them off with melee attacks. They're not tough at all, so a few good strikes should do the trick.

Continue breaking through battle droid soldiers until you encounter a super battle droid. Rush behind the short wall on the left and take cover. Open fire on the super battle droid and drop it quickly before rushing past it, deeper into the city.

Vault over the fallen rubble and lead your men deeper into the city. Storm up the walkway to another small ledge, then leap over it and back down to the other side. Hop down to the left into a small bunkerlike area.

Take cover behind the short wall and join your men in obliterating the oncoming droid forces. Stay behind your wall and use grenades to quickly demolish the enemy forces as they approach. If the grenades don't do the trick, switch back to your blaster and finish off whichever droids your grenades left behind.

After you dispatch the first wave of enemies, a second wave appears from the left and the right; some of them are perched atop a series of rooftops. The enemies on the rooftops pose more of a threat than those on the street, since they're shooting from an elevated position. Open fire on them first, then turn on the droids in the street.

Hold position at the next short wall in the alley ahead and open fire on the battle droids. After destroying them, rush out of cover and into the next open courtyard. The area is blanketed in blaster fire; unfortunately, you can't fire on the enemy from the safety of the alley.

Rush out of the alley, kicking and swinging as you destroy the first few battle droids in the courtyard. After taking them out, rush to the right, toward a small open room where the super battle droids' blaster fire can't reach you.

 **NOTE**

Another Droid Demolition mission challenge pops up after eliminating all of the enemies in this area.

 TIP

You can also approach this courtyard by simply exiting the alley and blasting the battle droids on the right while the super battle droids walk down the stairs. If you're fast enough, you'll take out the battle droids before they set up and while the super battle droids are still on the stairs.

Once the area is free of Separatist forces, rush out of your cover and dash down the street ahead. Leap over the

short wall in the street, then open fire on the next few battle droids in your way. This stuns them and softens

ARTIFACT

An artifact is inside the small room on the courtyard's right side. Sneak in and grab it before leaving the area.

Sneak out of cover and rush the super battle droids. Take them out, sprint up the steps behind them, and enter the next battlefield. This one is a large, circular area with a fountain in the center. Take cover behind the short wall on the right and open fire on the battle droids in your way. Once they're out of the way, vault over the wall and grab some more explosive grenades from the explosive-grenade station on the other side.

PSP NOTES

In the PSP version, you deal with only normal battle droids in this area.

TIP

If you plan ahead, you can refrain from using your thermal detonator until you get up the stairs. Use it on the group on the right to clear the blaster fire and resupply at the pick-up location. Save the thermal detonators for large groups, as they will quickly gun you down. Kneel and use your blaster on distant enemies whenever possible, but make the closer, more dangerous ones your top priority.

Follow your men up and around the yard. Position yourself behind the large, square structure on the yard's right edge and toss an explosive grenade at the super battle droid perched atop the distant building.

Make a right down the yard, taking cover behind the next short wall. From here, you can see the rooftops on the left, the distant archway from which more droids pour out, and the left edge of the fountain. Aim at the droids on the distant rooftops and open fire!

After destroying the droids on the rooftops, dash to the right and enter the fountain interior. Restock on explosive grenades as you enter, then grab cover to the statue's left. Aim explosive grenades at the droidekas on the far left. Let the grenades fly and disrupt the droidekas' shields. Once their shields are down, open fire with your blaster and destroy them.

Restock on grenades quickly, then rush toward the center of the fountain's border. Aim a grenade at the archway at the yard's opposite end and wait for more waves of droids to come marching out. As soon as they poke their heads out of the archway, let your grenade fly and blow them up.

Hold your position at the center and continue to greet the oncoming droids with grenades and blaster fire.

With the area clear, your men canvas the area. One of them finds a droid holo-communicator and eavesdrops on two droids' conversation. The droids reveal the presence of several more outposts on the planet! When you relay the message to Anakin Skywalker, he vows to send reinforcements and promises to join you as you explore the rest of the sector.

Rookie Rendezvous: Ryloth-Mission 4

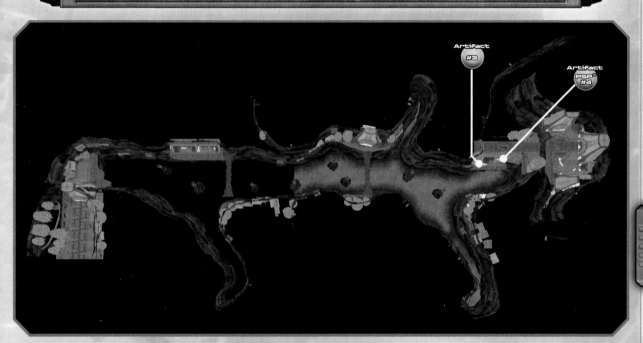

After a short while, Anakin Skywalker and Ahsoka arrive to help the clone troops. As always, the Jedi Knight is calm and ready for battle, while his Padawan is eager for a good fight.

A STAP Joy Ride, This Is Not

As Ahsoka, sneak up behind the two STAP-riding droids and double-jump out and onto one of the vehicles. Hijack the vehicle and ride it across the chasm, blasting the battle droid troop in your way.

NOTE

Rather than take control of Anakin Skywalker, you take control of Ahsoka during this mission. Have at 'em!

PSP AND WII NOTES

In the PSP and Wii versions, the STAPs are in the next room after the doorway, and there are no droids on them.

NOTE

A lot of this mission takes place while on a STAP vehicle. You'll be constantly in motion as you move left and right along the path, dodging or destroying obstacles and collecting point spheres. Of course, you don't have to collect the point spheres, but what's the fun in that?

Pass through the archway on the STAP and drift left with your blasters ablaze. Destroy the first pillar and grab the point spheres floating directly behind it. Immediately drift right toward the next pillar and destroy it, grabbing the point spheres behind it. Speed past the droids on the left, and shift toward the center of the cliffs.

The next pillar emits a dangerous electrical field across the cliff side, blocking your path. Let Anakin watch your back while you take aim and fire at the generator emitting the electrical field. Destroy the generator to stop the electrical field, then continue on your way.

NOTE

A Droid Demolition challenge pops up as soon as you destroy the generator.

PSP AND WII NOTES

In the Wii and PSP versions, no electrical field will be blocking your path, and the mission challenge is not present.

The next area is a bit tricky to maneuver if you want to get all the point spheres. Move all the way to the left and destroy the next pillar. Grab all the point spheres, then immediately drift right toward the next pillar. Follow the trail of point spheres back toward the cliff's left side, then destroy the droids perched along the left-side cliff.

Once again, destroy the next pillar on the left before drifting back toward the right and collecting more point spheres. Smash the next bridge before you reach it, and follow the point sphere trails from the center of the path back toward the left.

The next two rows of point spheres are too far apart from each other to grab both, so quickly drift right and line yourself up with the pillar on the right. Blow it up, then follow the long, crooked point-sphere path from the right, back to the left.

Blast past the next few droids guarding the bridge ahead, then shift all the way to the right. Crumble another pillar before grabbing some more point spheres and following them back to the path's left side. Bust through two more pillars and reach another electrical field generator blocking your path.

Just as before, let Anakin handle the droids that attack from behind while you focus on destroying the generator and eliminating the electrical field.

NOTE

As soon as you destroy the field generator, a Point Panic challenge pops up nearby. To get some tips on how to beat it, see the "Point Panic Tips" section in the Ways of the Force chapter.

PSP AND WII NOTES

In the Wii and PSP versions, there will not be a generator or mission challenge present in this location.

Destroy the super battle droids on the next bridge, then dash past the rubble toward another pair of tall pillars.

After passing them, turn left into the next area and disembark.

Jump on top of the building on the right, then dash up the incline toward the break in the platform above you. Double-jump onto the platform above and grab the edge of the walkway. Follow it left and right to grab all the point spheres, then hoist yourself back up.

ARTIFACT

An artifact is located at the walkway's far left ledge. Go to the far wall and follow the point spheres to the corner of the area to the artifact.

PSP NOTES

In the PSP version, the artifact is the first object to the left of the break in the walkway.

Sneak up to the super battle droids on the right and droid-jack one of them. While on the super battle droid, fire at the other droids across the chasm on the right. Take them all out before hopping off your toy robot and creeping on to the thin beam sticking out of the chasm.

Grab the power-up, then double-jump to the other side of the gap. Dash toward the battle droids on the left and hit them with a Force Blast. When you do, a small wave of super battle droids busts out of the door on the right. Either take them out with a few Force Blasts or droid-jack one of them and turn it into a weapon. Destroy the final wave of super battle droids and complete your mission!

PSP NOTES

In the PSP version, a power-up will not be present. Also, you'll need to destroy the entire first wave of battle droids before the next one shows up. The next wave will approach from the door in the back.

Assault! Juma-9-Mission 1

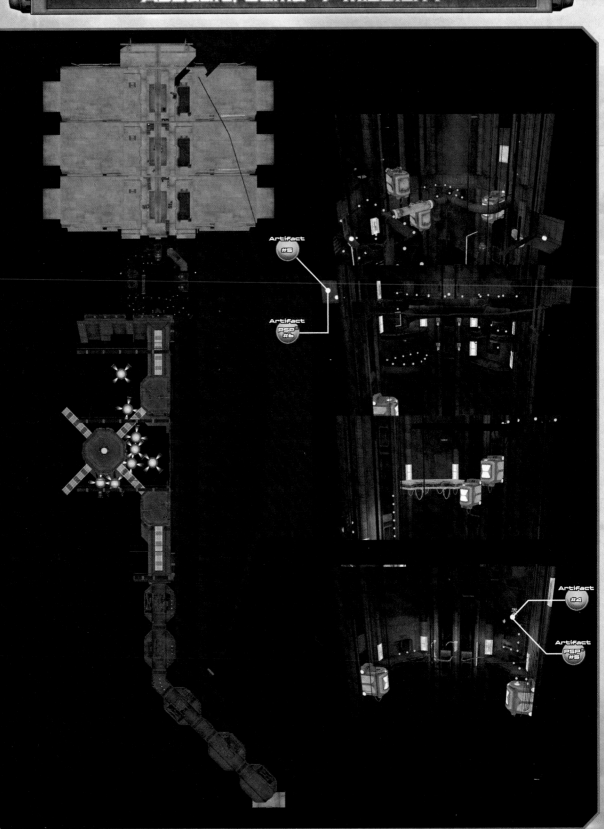

36

While Anakin, Ahsoka, and the Republic forces take care of business on Ryloth, Master Kenobi stops at the Juma-9 space station to refuel his starfighter. While there, he decides to speak with the station commander. En route to the commander's office, he runs into Jedi Master Plo Koon, who has not heard about the rumors concerning a possible Separatist presence on Naboo.

The two Jedi Masters walk side by side toward the commander's office and are rudely interrupted while in the elevator. As the elevator rises, the Jedi sense a disturbance in the Force. The space station has been infiltrated by Separatist forces!

NOTE

During this mission, you take control of Master Kenobi.

No Match for Masters, Droids Are

Upon exiting the elevator, rush up the corridor to the closed sliding door. Repeated Force Blast the door to open it, then speed into the next corridor. As you do, a small squad of battle droids drops in from above! Blast through them,

then turn left, where another hatch slides open and more battle droids come storming out.

Slash through them, then turn right. Sprint through the next hatch, across the holo-bridge, and into the next corridor. As you enter, a wall explodes as an attack pod bursts forth, taking out two super battle droids and depositing a more dangerous destroyer droid. Hop onto the platform on the right, collect the point spheres, then double-jump left past the burning debris.

Grab the point spheres on the platform to your right; then Force Blast the droideka off the ledge ahead of you.

Walk up to the ledge. From there, you see a pair of clone troopers across the gap. They activate the holo-bridge

and welcome you across. Grab the point spheres in the next small room, then open the next hatch. Another group of battle droids waits to ambush you! Dash into their ranks and take them out with a few well-placed lightsaber strikes.

When the super battle droids arrive, hop atop one of them and droid-jack it. Guide it around the area as you blast the remaining droids, then hop off as more droids storm in from the left. Cut them down with your lightsaber, and grab the power-up from atop the crates on the left.

TIP

This is a good area in which to get the Double Trouble Achievement, as your partner can also hop on top of a super battle droid.

37

PRIMAGAMES.COM

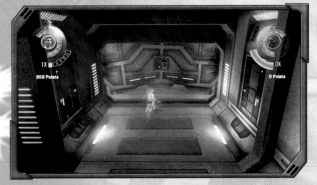

Destroy the droid in the next corridor, then Force Blast the next hatch open. The hatch doesn't open all the way, but it does pop up just enough for you to slide underneath it. Do as Master Yoda says and run toward the door; slide under it to get past.

PSP NOTES

In the PSP version, the hatch opens all the way for you.

Dash across the next holo-bridge and hop on the floating platform on the other side. Ride it up to the next level of the station. As you ride the platform, Master Plo Koon expresses his doubts about winning the battle against the attacking Separatists.

When you reach the next level, throw your lightsaber and cut through the surrounding droids. Hold your position on the circular platform and wait for another floating elevator to pop up nearby. When they do, stand back and wait for the droids to cross the red holo-bridges to your platform. Greet them with lightsaber combos. You can also use a Force Blast to clear each bridge before the droids have a chance to fire.

CAUTION

Do not step on the red holo-bridges! They will deplete your health if you set foot on them.

Fend off the first few waves of droids until a pair of droideka attack! Hit them with a Force Blast and knock them off your platform before they can cause any harm. When the final two super battle droids drop down from above, either slash through them with your lightsaber or droid-jack one of them and destroy the other.

NOTE

After surviving all of the droid waves, a Knockback Knockout challenge appears on your platform. For tips on how to beat the challenge, see the "Knockback Knockout Tips" section in the Ways of the Force chapter.

PSP NOTES

In the PSP version, no droideka attack you, and there is no mission challenge.

Cross the new holo-bridge on the left. This leads to a small floating platform and a doorway with the same clones you've been fighting with. It then disappears, dropping you onto a pipe below. Hop onto the sabotage droid that appears here, and use it to break the weakened wall.

PSP AND WII NOTES

In the Wii and PSP versions, the hole in the wall is already present, and there aren't any droids to battle.

Leap through the hole in the wall. Jump onto the walkway on the right and follow it down to a series of poles and pipes. From here, you can either swing across the jutting poles or follow the twisting pipe at your feet to the next area.

TIP

Each route has point spheres to collect. If you want to get them all, creep out on the pipe at your feet, then double back and swing across the jutting poles.

ARTIFACT

Once you've crossed onto the other side, hoist yourself into the small niche in the wall behind you. Inside is an artifact!

Jump atop the small elevator on the right and ride it up to the next walkway. As you pull up to it, the walkway explodes, creating a gap. Use the small floating platforms in the gap to hop across, then jump atop the next malfunctioning elevator, which rises and drops while another next to it does the same.

Carefully jump from one elevator to the next, then hop off the second lift by jumping onto the thick pipe nearby. From here, you can either follow the pipe or traverse the small ledge along the left wall to a series of poles. Swing across to another platform.

Jump into the small niche, then bound up the walls to the next level. Leap onto the long plank on the left and follow it left. Double-jump onto the next plank and to the next platform. Wall-bound up the next small niche to the level above.

ARTIFACT

Though your path leads you right, stop after climbing the last niche and make a left to find another artifact. Hop across the two small platforms onto the ledge in the wall. Follow it to a hole in the wall, where an artifact is located.

Make a right after bounding up the niche and step onto the thick pipe jutting out of the wall. Follow the pipe until it forks. If you take the right path, you'll find a power-up. The left path leads to several point spheres perched above a ledge. Follow them to a niche hiding a point crystal, then out to another thick pipe.

39

Just as before, the pipe splits into two directions. One leads out and around while the other path leads to the wall with more point spheres. Follow either path to the next elevator and hop on top of it. Take the elevator up to the next level, and go through the door behind you. A fierce battle rages on in the next area. Join your men and rush out into battle with your lightsaber swinging!

Droid-jack one of the super battle droids nearby, and turn it on the approaching waves of weaker battle droids. Blast through the first few waves of droids as you sprint to the left. Hop onto the cargo crates on the walkway's far edge, grab the red power-up, and hop back down. Demolish the droids in your way, then leap onto the near edge of the walkway, where you find more point spheres.

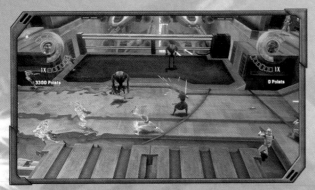

Grab the spheres and hop down onto the walkway to ambush several more droid troops. A platform rises from the walkway's far edge, delivering more super battle droids to the fight. Let Plo Koon handle some of the weaker droids while you attack the super battle droids.

NOTE

After fending off the waves of droids, a Takeover Takedown challenge becomes available. For tips on how to beat it, see the "Takeover Takedown Tips" section in the Ways of the Force chapter.

PSP NOTES

This mission challenge is not available in the PSP version.

Continue left to fight off another wave of droids while collecting the last few point spheres on this walkway. Droid-jack a super battle droid and take out the smaller droids nearby. When the two droideka roll in, double-jump into the air and use a slam attack to disable their shields. With their shields gone, double-jump again and droid-jack one of them. Target it at the other droideka and let it loose!

PSP NOTES

The two droideka are not present in the PSP version.

When you reach the end of the walkway, you find a dead end and several more droideka! You order Commander Cody to divert all power to the station's deflector shields, but he's got some bad news. Droids have breached the reactor core! You promise to take care of them while he and his men head for the control room to try and reinforce the shields.

Power Reroute: Juma-9-Mission 2

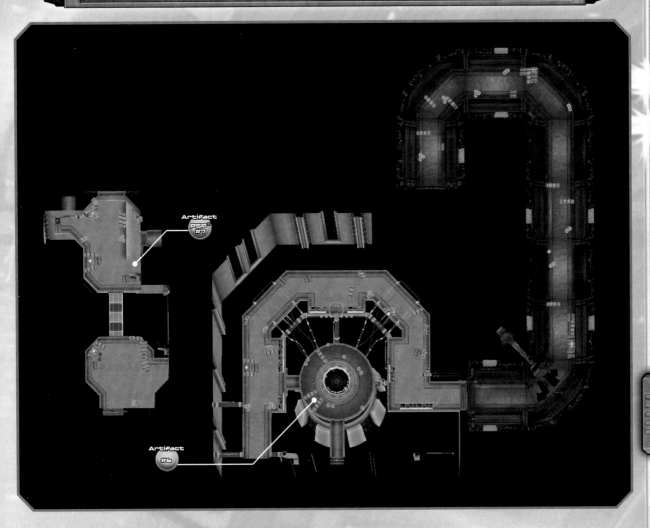

Artifact
PSP
#7

Artifact
#6

While Jedi Masters Obi-Wan Kenobi and Plo Koon set out to the reactor core, a small squad of clone soldiers head out to reinforce the deflector shields. The four-man squad is ready for battle!

NOTE

During this mission, you take control of a clone trooper.

Dangerous, a Clone Soldier's Job Is

Head right and stock up on explosive grenades. Approach the console on the right and activate it. You'll need to short-circuit the conduit by lining up the green sections of the ring. Once you do, the holo-bridge activates and grants you access to the next area.

41

PRIMAGAMES.COM

Don't cross right away. Instead, wait for the battle droid squad to march across the bridge. As it does, lob a grenade at them. Shoot the remaining attacking droids, then rush across the bridge, grabbing the red power-up on the left.

Strafe right, across the platform as more droids come in. Blast them as they approach. Rush up the small elevated walkway on the right and take out the super battle droid by the next computer console.

Hold your position for a while as you fight off two small droid waves that attack from the right; then use the computer console. Hack it by lining up all three ring sections; this opens the far hatch. Sprint through into the next corridor, and take out the two super battle droids on the right.

Stock up on grenades again and strafe back and forth on the walkway. Toss a few grenades at the squad of droids farther down the corridor until you destroy them; then take the fight to the battle droids that remain.

Follow the walkway as it turns right and drops down into a decline, then hurl one more grenade at the gold super battle droids ahead. Wait for the electrical bursts emanating from the wall to stop; when they do, rush past the malfunctioning wall panel.

NOTE

These wall panels become active only if you shoot them.

PSP NOTES

The gold super battle droid is not present in the PSP version.

With no more crates to provide cover on the ramp, strafe back and forth down the ramp with your rifle blaster ablaze. Gun down the battle droids ahead, and veer left when you reach the bottom. Climb atop the stack of crates on the left, and replace your explosive grenades with a rocket launcher!

PSP NOTES

The rocket launcher will be on the ground in the PSP version.

From the top of the crates, fire a rocket at the debris ahead and blow it up! Hop down, dash past the fallen debris, and replace your rocket launcher with explosive grenades from the next station. Vault over the crates on the ground and hack the next computer console on the right. This console has red rings too—if you line them up, they'll polarize and you'll have to start all over again!

HACK!

To hack this console, first move the smallest, innermost green ring right so that the red ring section is facing the top right and the small green ring section is facing the top left. Once that is in place, move the medium green ring section all the way right, until it lines up with the large green ring section. Then return to the small green ring section and move it right one more time until all three green ring sections are lined up.

PSP NOTES

In the PSP version, move the small green ring right two times so that they all line up.

Sprint into the next section of the station, and immediately take cover behind the crates. Either toss grenades at the battle droids across from you or fire at them with your blaster rifle. After you deal with them, rush out from your cover and hack the console near the area's center.

HACK!

To hack this console, first move the second green ring section right once, lining it up with the large green ring section. Then simply turn the third green ring section left until it, too, lines up with the other green ring sections. Don't bother moving the smallest green ring section.

PSP NOTES

To slice this console in the PSP version, move the topmost ring right once and the innermost ring right once.

The console routes power away from the electrical field on the right and into the deflector shields! With the electrical fields down, rush right along the walkway toward the next few crates. Grab some cover behind them and open fire on the droids ahead.

Clear them out, then approach the next computer console. Before using the console, grab some grenades from the station nearby. Hack the console to remove the next electrical field and reroute it to the deflector shields. In addition to the green ring sections, this console also has blue sections. In order to activate it, line up the green and blue ring sections. Crush the destroyer droids that appear while you're hacking the console.

HACK!

To hack this console, first move the second green ring section—which is also attached to the first blue ring section—and line it up with the large green ring section. This moves the first blue ring section to the bottom left. Then, rotate the small blue ring section to line up with the larger one.

NOTE

By activating the second console, you also unlock a Droid Demolition challenge!

PSP NOTES

In the PSP version, slice this console by moving the outer ring to the left once and the inner ring to the right once. Also, the mission challenge is not available in the PSP version.

Storm down the walkway ahead, over crates and other small obstacles, then replace your grenades with a rocket launcher from the station on the left. Open fire on the droideka that attack from across the walkway, and grab the red power-up floating high above the crate stack on the right. From there, obliterate the rest of the attacking droids, then hop down and reload your rocket launcher.

Once the waves of droids subside, come down from your elevated position and make a left toward the inner ring, where the next console is located. Hack the final console by lining up the green and blue ring sections.

After hacking all three consoles, the power is rerouted to the deflector shields. When you report mission success to Master Kenobi, he orders you and the rest of your men to secure the docking section and the cargo decks.

HACK!

To hack this console, first move the second green section right once to line it up with the large green section. This also moves the first blue ring section to the top right position. Finally, move the second blue ring section left until it lines up with the other blue ring section.

ARTIFACT

An artifact is located on the right side of the inner ring. Grab it before you hack the final console!

PSP NOTES

In the PSP version, the red power-up is located next to the terminal on the other side. To slice the console, move the first ring to the right once and the middle ring to the left. Also, the artifact is located after the first holo-bridge, behind the crates on the right side.

44

PRIMA OFFICIAL GAME GUIDE

Hazardous Infestation: Juma-9-Mission 3

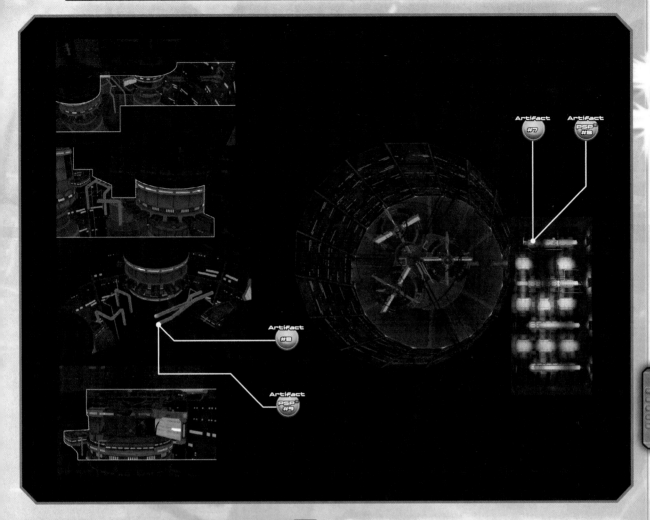

45

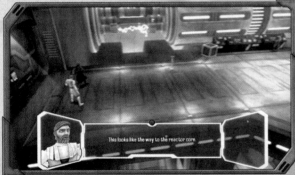

The trusty clone troopers got the job done as always. With the deflector shield back up to full power, the only thing left to do is clear out the hazardous infestation of Separatist troops inside the Juma-9 space station! With the plan clearly laid out, Jedi Masters Obi-Wan Kenobi and Plo Koon set off toward the reactor core to clean house.

NOTE

During this mission, you take control of Plo Koon!

In the Shadows, the Dark Side Always Lurks

Follow the walkway right until a chameleon droid ambushes you. Dodge its attacks while grabbing the point spheres scattered atop the two computer console stations; then double-jump from the console station to the top of the chameleon droid while it's exposed. Crush the cowardly droid, and proceed farther down the walkway.

When you come across the mines on the ground, Force Push them away before proceeding. Next, do as Master Yoda suggests and slide underneath the next few chameleon droids while slashing them from below. If they lay more mines, Force Push them away before slashing the droids to bits. Force Pushing the mines while below the droids and performing jump attacks are very good ways of dealing with the chameleon droids too.

Crush the next two chameleon droids on the last part of the walkway, and hop left toward the next turbine. Swing onto the turbine platform, then step out onto the connecting pipe. Jump down onto the walkway below and slide underneath the chameleon droid when it appears. Slice the droid from below as you slide under it to destroy it.

Once the area is clear, jump atop the computer console on the right, then double-jump onto the pipe next to it. Grab the small pole and swing from it onto the large spinning turbine. Walk across the turbine platform, launch yourself to the nearby pole, and swing onto the next large pipe and back down to the platform on the turbine's other side.

Double-jump up the series of pipes onto the next turbine platform. Make a left and follow the walkway, destroying mines as you go.

Grab the pole at the walkway's end and launch yourself onto the pipes high above the next platform. Follow the pipes across, then jump down onto the walkway below. If you want to grab the point crystal underneath the pipes, throwing your lightsaber at it or approaching it from the pipes below could help you reach it.

Edge out onto the large protruding beam, then turn left to face the pipe in the distance. Double-jump onto the pipe, and follow it right. When you reach the next stable section of the walkway, jump from the pipe back onto the walkway. Force Push the mines over the ledge, and break the point crystal nearby as you battle the chameleon droid. Destroy the disappearing droid, then either hop across the small floating platforms or cross the long beam onto the next section of walkway on the right.

Jump from the turbine onto the large pipe on the turbine's left; follow the pipe toward the next walkway area. Jump across the two pipes until you're within jumping distance of the walkway below.

TIP

There are several point spheres on this pipe. Explore the length of the pipe to grab them all!

ARTIFACT

There is another artifact nearby! After jumping off the turbine platform onto the large pipe, follow the pipe up to its end. Look right and find the artifact on a small platform.

Make a sharp left as soon as you reach the circular platform. Run toward the small pole sticking out from the platform's side. Rather than swing on the pole, leap into the small niche in the platform. Run your lightsaber through the console in the niche, and the force fields rotate slightly around the platform.

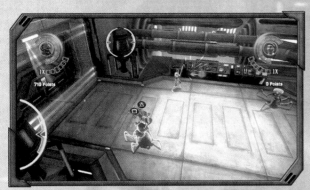

Upon landing on the walkway, a pair of chameleon droids appears! Don't slash them from below.

Instead, droid-jack them and direct them toward the large red generators powering the force field nearby. As you pass the generators, drop mines from the droid and detonate them.

When the generators explode, the force field comes down. Pass through the doorway, then leap across the small floating platforms to the next section of walkway. The demolished walkway leads to a large circular platform with several red force fields around it.

Once the fields have rotated left, swing from the nearby pole onto the next catwalk on the left. Follow it to another niche, and slice the next console to rotate the fields again. Follow the small ledge out of the niche, then leap back onto the next platform. From there, leap across the next two pipes to a series of platforms that pop in and out of the next circular structure.

Time your jumps accordingly so that when the platform underneath turns red, you're in the air and on your way to the next platform. If you stand on the platform too long, it'll recede back into the structure and send you free-falling! The platform gives you a second or two before it pulls back, which can help you with your timing.

PSP NOTES

There are no red generators in the PSP version.

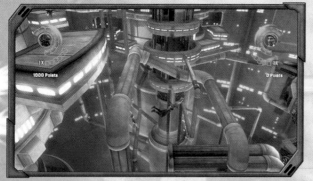

Upon reaching the end of the moving platforms, launch yourself onto the two small curved pipes on the left. Swing across the poles, moving left as you go, then stop on the second pole and turn around. Spring toward the platform on the right, just above your head, and turn around one more time to jump onto the pipe on the left.

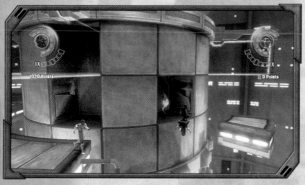

On the next circular structure, the force fields are high above you and are constantly rotating. Sneak into the niche in the structure and grab the point spheres inside. Creep out onto the thin pipe jutting from the right of the catwalk, and wait for the force field overhead to pass you. When it does, leap onto the small floating platform and let it carry you to the next catwalk section.

From the next small catwalk, turn right and jump onto the thick pipe. Either follow it out to another pipe or swing from the nearby pole onto the next pipe. Both routes lead to a small ledge with a computer console on it. Ram your lightsaber into the console; this sets the moving platforms lining the structure into motion.

These platforms pop in and out, just as the previous platforms did on the earlier structure. Quickly leap across the platforms before they move away from underneath your feet until you reach another small pipe on the right. The first time the platform comes out, it gives you plenty of time. Use this to your advantage!

Follow the thin pipe to another large pipe, and use the small platforms floating ahead of you to reach the next circular structure.

PSP NOTES

There is no force field above here in the PSP version.

TIP

As you float safely across the gap in the catwalk, you can leap into the hole on the structure's left to get a point crystal!

ARTIFACT

After reaching the thick pipe, follow it right to a large round barrel, where an artifact waits to be collected. Then use the small platforms to reach the next circular structure.

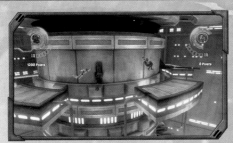

Follow the poles and catwalks right, around the large circular structure until you reach a red force field blocking your path. Use the floating platform to rise above the force field and reach the circular platform above you.

When you set foot on the next level, the force fields begin to rotate to the right. Follow the catwalks right, staying ahead of the force fields and destroying the mines in your way with Force Push. Stop only to destroy the chameleon droids that appear, then quickly get back on the move to stay ahead of the deadly force fields!

TIP

Pay close attention to the outer rings just outside the structure. Though they occasionally come to life with dangerous electricity, they also have valuable point spheres and power-ups to grab when they're not electrified!

Follow the catwalk to its end. When the fields stop rotating, turn right and use the little flying platform to

reach the next circular structure on the right. This time, the force fields force you to flee to the left! Run away from the rotating fields and fend off a few more feisty chameleon droids.

NOTE

After destroying the first few droids on this structure, a Point Panic challenge appears.

PSP NOTES

This mission challenge is not present in the PSP version.

Turn left when the fields stop rotating again, and use the floating platforms nearby to reach another structure in the distance. Turn left on the new structure and run away from the rotating force fields. Force Push the mines away and destroy the chameleon droids that attack.

Don't use slide attacks, since you'll risk sliding into the force field. Instead, droid-jack them and crush them from above or use Force Pushes to push them off the structure. Clear out the last few chameleon droids to clean the reactor core of all enemy presence.

With the area clear, Plo Koon attempts to contact Anakin Skywalker, only to find the Separatists

have jammed communications! The only way to reach Skywalker and Tano is to use the station's high-power transmitters to send out a signal.

PRIMA OFFICIAL GAME GUIDE

Seek and Destroy: Ryloth-Mission 5

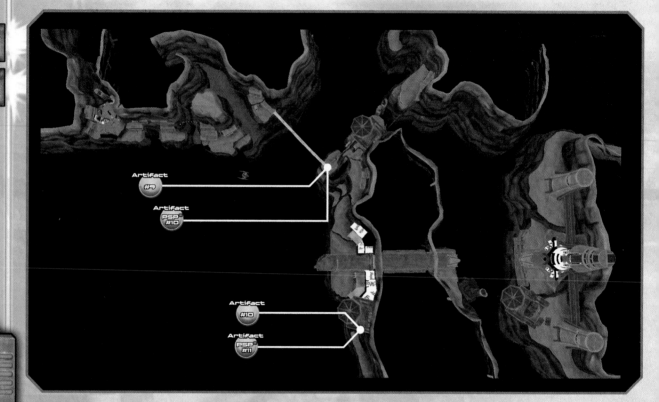

50

Back on Ryloth, Anakin and Ahoska continue to work with the clone troops to clean the planet of Separatist forces. As they travel across the city of Resdin, Ahsoka senses a tremor in the Force. With no concrete clue as to what it is, the duo can do nothing until the tremor gets worse. For now, they must continue to clear the outposts.

NOTE

During this mission, you take control of Anakin Skywalker.

Dug in Deep, the Separatists Are

The Separatists have dug themselves deep in the city. Before attacking the nearest droid soldiers, grab the point crystal in the nearby house, then sneak up on the droid troops below. Droid-jack the super battle droid below and blast the battle droids stationed nearby. If you miss landing on the super battle droid's head, use Force Blasts or Force Kill to knock them off the cliff.

After you take out the droid squad, a spider droid crawls up to the edge of the cliff across from you, while more super battle droids march out of the surrounding buildings. Destroy the super battle droid that emerges from the passage above you, along the cliff-side wall. Then use the passage to cross the chasm and reach the spider droid.

PSP AND WII NOTES

In the Wii and PSP versions, there is no super battle droid, and you'll use ropes to cross the chasm instead of a passage.

Droid-jack the spider droid and use it to destroy the super battle droids across the small chasm. When a second spider droid crawls up the cliff side, droid-jack it, too, and aim it at the large pillar behind you. After you destroy the pillar, two groups of super battle droids march in from behind you and on the other side of the busted pillar.

PSP AND WII NOTES

In the Wii and PSP versions, there will be no super battle droid present across the chasm, and the second spider droid

Jump atop the pillar, then onto the other side of the cliff. Take out the two super battle droids, then take the fight to the small battle droid battalion. Knock them off the cliff, then double-jump onto the spider droid that crawls up behind you. Droid-jack it, then blow up the small shack on the cliff's right side.

When you do, a control console is exposed inside the busted shack. Take out the remaining droids in the area, then use the Force to activate the holo-bridge leading to the next area. Rush across the bridge, and smash the super battle droids on the other side.

PSP AND WII NOTES

In the Wii and PSP versions, there are no super battle droids or spider droids.

WII NOTES

In the Wii version, you can simply run over and hit the switch to activate the bridge.

PSP NOTES

In the PSP version, the bridge will already be activated.

Jump atop the buildings along the left cliff side and take out the spider droid. Next, turn your attention toward the approaching battle droids at the right and destroy them. As you do, Ahsoka will follow suit and attack the waves of battle droids. Leave her to it while you go and destroy the two super battle droids that approach from the left.

Dash across the next bridge. When you do, a vulture droid bombs it, destroying the bridge beneath you. Continue moving forward until a rocket-firing droid ambushes you from a distance. Wait for it to launch rockets at you, then bounce them back at it to destroy the droid. Two more appear and can be taken out with the same process.

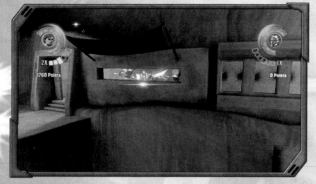

Finish crossing the bridge, and grab the Invincibility power-up nearby. Dash into the passage along the right cliff side and fight your way through it, destroying several droids along the way. Exit the passage, then swing across the next gap onto a small pillar.

PSP NOTES

In the PSP version, there are no vulture droids, and you'll progress through this area by crossing a series of pillars. No Invincibility power-up is present, but there is an artifact after the pillar area to the right of the house on the ledge.

Hop across the pillars to the next platform, high atop a cliff.

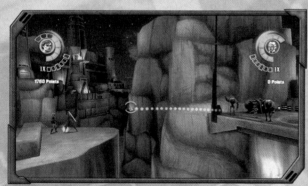

Turn right and locate the next batch of droids across the chasm. Raise your lightsaber to block their blaster fire

and wait for one of them to launch a rocket at you. When they do, lower your lightsaber and knock the rocket back toward them. The rocket destroys the droid squad and brings down a long antenna that then bridges the gap between the chasm.

Sprint across the fallen antenna to the other cliff side. Run your lightsaber through the super battle droids on the other side and dash toward the chameleon droids and battle droids that emerge from the small building on the steps above. You must defeat all of these enemies before you can move on.

Jump atop the building, then hoist yourself up into the area above you. Turn right and jump down into the area below. Rush the battle droids stationed in front of the large red force field and bust them to bits. Droid-jack the super battle droid that appears from the small building on the right, then turn it on the battle droids that attack from the small bridge on the cliff's near end.

Jump onto the roof of the building on the right and turn left. Use the sabotage droids as floating platforms and hop across them as you move left across the area, past the red force field. Demolish the super battle droids on the building to the left of the force field, then follow the point spheres up and around the cliff side.

PSP AND WII NOTES

In the Wii and PSP versions, you'll pass a large metal door instead of a red force field.

PSP NOTES

In the PSP version, the holo-bridge is already on when you enter the room.

Follow the point spheres right, back across the area and over the red force field. When you reach the next large octagonal platform, jump onto a destroyer droid and jack it! Ride it over to the generator on the left. Before blasting the generator, collect an artifact inside the explosive barrels. When the generator blows up, the red force field below deactivates.

PSP AND WII NOTES

In the Wii and PSP versions, you'll use swing props to get over the large metal door, and there is an artifact next to the console to the right of it. Also, to lower the door, you will slice a console, which is guarded by super battle droids.

NOTE

After deactivating the red force field, a Droid Demolition challenge appears in the area below.

Jump to the area below and go through the now-open passage. On the passage's other side, a small group of jetpack-toting clone troopers swoops by. They fly ahead of you and activate the holo-bridge linking your walkway and the area ahead.

Storm across the bridge. As you do, your clone troopers come under heavy attack! Crush the droids on the bridge's other side, and locate the two generators flanking the tower ahead. Wait for two spider droids to crawl up the sides of the cliff, then droid-jack them.

Target the generators while riding the spider droids and destroy them! When you do, the Separatist-controlled tower explodes!

When the tower falls, your troops are saved. They survive the assault on the outpost but still require a medical evac to the plaza.

53

Emergency Evac: Ryloth—Mission 6

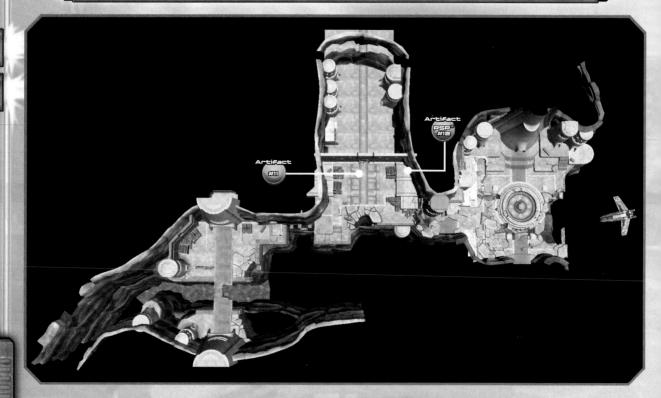

54

Once Anakin and his Padawan have been reunited with his clone soldiers, Anakin rushes his men to the plaza where they can be evacuated.

Left Behind, No Soldier Should Be

Rush across the small bridge on the right and wait for a squad of battle droids and super battle droids to march out of the doorway ahead. As your clone soldiers take cover behind the small crate stacks on the left and right, rush out and meet the droids head-on.

Support your clones' blaster fire with your lightsaber as you dash back and forth around the area, destroying droids as they approach. Droid-jack one of the super battle droids to make short work of the smaller, weaker battle droids. When the next few waves appear, leave your clone soldiers to cover the doorway while you cover their backs.

PSP NOTES

In the PSP version, there are four battle droids outside the doorway and two crab droids inside it.

Move right after fending off all the droid waves and approach the small gap between areas. Let your soldiers fire on the droideka across the gap while you grab the ledge on the left and wall-run across the gap by wall.

Follow the ledge across until you reach the power-up just below the droideka. Once you've grabbed the power-up, pull yourself up onto the ledge and knock the droideka off it. If you miss at first, keep trying! With the droideka gone, the clone soldiers can activate the holo-bridge and cross it.

PSP NOTES

In the PSP version, the droideka and power-up are not present here, and you'll use three ledges along the wall to get across the gap to attack a group of super battle droids.

WII NOTES

In the Wii version, you can continue through the area without destroying the droideka, whereas you must destroy this foe in other the versions.

Lead them right, around the next corner, and slash the droid soldiers waiting for you there. Use jump attacks and lightsaber combos to take them all out. When the spider droids decloak, droid-jack them and smash them from above. Force Pushes are another viable option.

Turn right and dash across the small courtyard toward the next batch of droids. Run your lightsaber through them and jump from crate to crate until you reach the top of the bunker on the far right. When the sabotage droids appear, use Force Blasts to knock them out of the sky.

Once you've destroyed all of the sabotage droids, a small swarm of crab droids bursts through the wall at the other end of the courtyard. Dodge their shock-wave attacks and droid-jack one of the crab droids.

PSP AND WII NOTES

There are no sabotage droids present in the Wii and PSP versions.

ARTIFACT

There is an artifact floating high above the courtyard. Use a crab droid to reach it.

PSP AND WII NOTES

In the Wii and PSP versions, the artifact is atop a building on the right side of this courtyard.

Use Force Kills and jump attacks on the rear of the crab droids for instant kills.

After enduring several waves of droids, droid-jack one more crab droid and approach the large hangar door on the right. Blast the door with a shock-wave attack. As the door comes crashing down, several more super battle droids march out with blasters firing away.

Either destroy them with your lightsaber or jack one of them and turn it on the other. Enter the large hangar and head through it to the next area.

NOTE

After using the crab droid to destroy the hangar door, a Point Panic challenge appears.

PSP AND WII NOTES

In the Wii and PSP versions, you won't use a crab droid to destroy the hangar door. Also, there's no mission challenge here.

Immediately after crossing the hangar and emerging in the plaza, turn left and grab the power-up nearby. Almost immediately, a group of battle droids attacks from the right. Lunge into their ranks and slice through them.

PSP AND WII NOTES

In the Wii and PSP versions, there's no power-up present, and the first droid to attack is a droideka.

Hold your ground as more droids march in, and use Force Blasts to bounce rockets back toward the droid on the  plaza's top left corner. Dash around the plaza destroying droids. You can use your men as shields, as they are invincible. Destroy the chameleon droids that appear next.

After a short while, super battle droids and crab droids attack from the right. Jack one of the crab droids and turn it on the other droids in the area. If you can't reach the super battle droids on the upper level, rush up the steps and blast them with jump attacks.

NOTE

After surviving the waves of droids, a Takeover Takedown challenge appears in the plaza.

PSP AND WII NOTES

In the Wii and PSP versions, battle droids, super battle droids, destroyer droids, and crab droids appear on the left side, the top left door, the middle door, and the doors on the ledge to the top right.

After clearing the area, an LAAT arrives. Get your men on the ship and get them out of there!

Out on Patrol: Ryloth-Mission 7

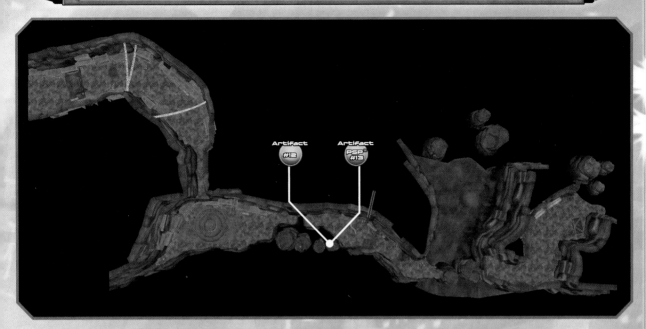

Artifact #12 Artifact PSP #13

Though the outposts have been nearly cleared out, Ryloth is still occupied by Separatist forces. One night, while out on patrol, two clone soldiers find more than they bargained for.

NOTE

This is a short but unique mission. You take control of a clone trooper while on an AT-RT vehicle.

Never Done, a Clone Trooper's Job Is

Stomp down the city streets and open fire as soon as you see the battle droids in the distance. Go up the ramp on the right, then make a right at the corner down the street.

Stay near the edges of the buildings as you fire on the droids farther down the street. If you take too much fire, back away and let your patrol partner handle the enemy forces ahead. Once you've recovered enough health, rejoin the battle!

First target the rocket-launching droids perched on the buildings to the right. After taking them out, rush down the street and wipe out the super battle droid guarding the small alley.

Pass through the narrow alley and leap down into the area below on the other side.

As soon as you land in the area below, two groups of droids attack, one from the right and another from the narrow alley you just passed through. Target the battle droids on the right first. Blow them to bits, then slink back toward the far wall.

When the spider droids crawl up the cliff side, rush out toward them and blast them. Take out the gold droid first, then turn on the super battle droids on the left. Sweep the area clear of all enemy droids, then prepare for a second wave.

No gold droid is present in the PSP version.

NOTE

Droid Demolition challenge appears after wiping the area clean of all enemy droids.

After destroying the second wave of enemies, stomp right, along the cliff side, and open fire on the enemies ahead. As you move left, either hug the cliff wall or leap from pillar to pillar until you reach the other side.

ARTIFACT

If you take the second route and hop across the pillars, be sure to grab the artifact on the last pillar.

Run down the steps on the right and demolish all the droids in your way. Jump onto the small pillar just off the chasm and wait for two STAP vehicles to approach. Destroy the STAP-riding droids, then finish jumping across the pillars to the next area.

Continue down the street, where you'll spy a shadow scurrying away. Give chase and finish your patrol.

Missing in Action: Ryloth-Mission 8

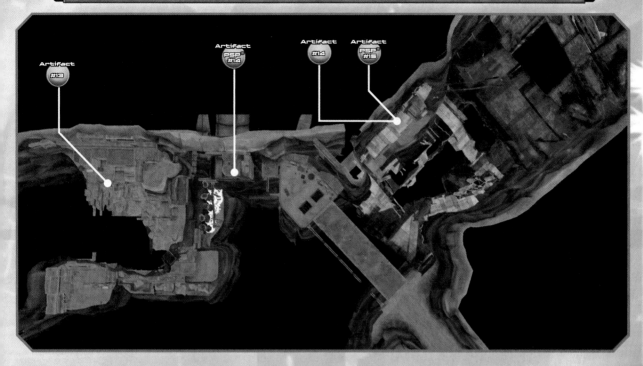

After completing their patrol, the clone troopers report to Anakin Skywalker. They've found something in the city and send him the coordinates. But before the clone soldier can identify what they've found, they come under attack.

The holo-transmission is interrupted, but not before Skywalker and Ahsoka get the troop's coordinates. If they're going to rescue their men, they must set out immediately!

Save His Soldiers, a General Must

Before setting out to save your men, break the point crystal nearby. Climb up the small incline along the far wall and follow it right. Jump onto the large concrete beam and gather point spheres as you travel along it.

Swing from the nearby pole onto the next concrete beam, and follow it down to a small circular area that has two more point crystals. Break the crystals and gather your points, then jump atop the nearby sabotage droid.

PSP AND WII NOTES

In the Wii and PSP versions, there are no point crystals until the end of this area, which you progress through by jumping from ruined building to ruined building.

NOTE

During this mission, you resume control of Anakin Skywalker.

Bound from the droid onto the long pipe behind it and follow the pipe up to a small pillar on its left. Bounce from the pipe to the pillar and then to the next ledge. Pull yourself up onto the next area and step inside the tall shaft in the building below. Bound all the way up. Break the point crystal floating above the shaft, then hop down on the other side.

PSP AND WII NOTES

In the Wii and PSP versions, the point crystal is replaced with an artifact, but in the PSP version, the Artifact is on top of the giant broken pipe.

Make a right past the shaft, then turn left when you near the concrete beams. Jump across the beams to the other side and collect the artifact in the niche on the right. Bounce up the niche, then edge out onto a small concrete beam.

ARTIFACT

You'll find an artifact at the base of the niche after crossing those two beams. Be sure to grab it before continuing.

Turn right on the beam, and swing from the nearby pole. Pull yourself up onto the pole, and turn left again to face

the ledge above and behind you. Jump onto the ledge to reach the next area. Break open the two point crystals in this area, then bounce up the niche along the far wall to reach the higher level.

PSP AND WII NOTES

In the Wii and PSP versions, use a swing prop to reach the ledge above, and then wall-jump back and forth to reach the top of the building. From here, head toward the big pipe.

Turn right again, and jump down on the other side of the building. Break the four point crystals, then leap across

the two pipes sticking out of the cliff side. Once you've reached the second pipe, hop all the way back down to the sloping area below.

Leap across the beams on the right until you reach an area with two large circular drainage grates along the wall. Two droideka roll out of the grates, and a spider droid emerges from the cliff side. Jack a droideka and use it to destroy the other droids.

NOTE

After taking down all the droids in this area, a Droid Demolition challenge appears near the center of the area.

PSP NOTES

In the PSP version, there's one Force crystal and two spider droids; there are no droideka. When all the droids have been defeated, you can continue on. Also, there is no mission challenge in this location.

Double-jump onto the long pipe in front of the bridge and follow it right to the next area. Jump left onto the platform and break open the two point crystals.

PSP AND WII NOTES

In the Wii and PSP versions, there's a broken bridge next to the pipe and no point crystals.

Walk to the top right corner of the area and slide left, down the long decline. After reaching the bottom, climb onto the platform along the far wall, and swing right onto a small platform jutting out from the wall. Break the point crystal on the platform, then either double-jump straight onto the next beam or double-jump right onto the pipe.

PSP NOTES

No point crystal is present in the PSP version.

Follow either path to a small platform with a pipe hanging overhead. Bounce off the far wall and back onto the pipe over the platform. Turn around as you swing on the pipe, then launch yourself onto the raised area behind you. Break the point crystal, then slide down the long decline on the right.

Double-jump across the small gap, and break open the point crystal on the other side. Turn right and carefully leap across the small barrel-like objects toward the next raised area.

PSP NOTES

No point crystal is present in the PSP version.

Swing across the two poles on the right until you land on the broken platform ahead. Go right along the cliff side until you reach a tall platform with poles in front of it. Swing from the first pole toward the platform and launch yourself into the wall. Bounce off the wall and grab the next pole, which is higher along the wall.

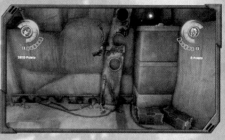

Turn around, then hoist yourself on top of the pole. From here, leap atop the platform.

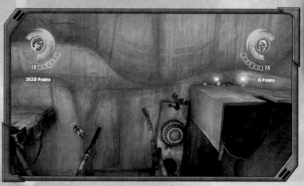

Turn left and leap out toward the next pole. Swing from it to a second pole just out of reach. Climb atop the pole, then turn around. Launch yourself at the pole above you, then swing onto the platform on the right.

ARTIFACT

Rather than turning around while on the second pole, launch yourself forward to a small platform just to the left. It has an artifact on it! Grab it, then return to the pole before resuming your journey.

Dash right along the walkway. When the ground gives way at your feet, you fall to the area below. There, two magna guards pounce! Let Ahsoka handle one while you take on the other. Wait for the guard to stop spinning its light staff, then attack it with a lightsaber combo.

61

PRIMAGAMES.COM

If the magna guard begins spinning its weapon again, back away until it stops, then resume your attack. You can also droid-jack one of the magna guards just as you would other droids—leap atop its head, jack it, then use it against the other guard!

After destroying the magna guards, you sense that Obi-Wan and Plo Koon are in danger. Unfortunately, your clone soldiers need you more than the two Jedi Masters. Your men are just beyond the rise ahead....You're almost there.

S.O.S: Juma-9-Mission 4

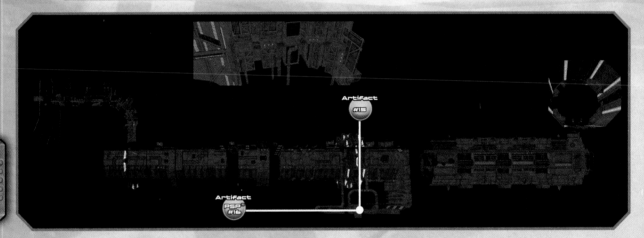

Reestablish Communications, You Must

While Anakin and Ahsoka set out to rescue their men, Masters Obi-Wan and Plo Koon are still on the Juma-9 space station. Unfortunately, the station is still overrun with droids, and the communications room is still a ways off.

Sprint right down the corridors and leap over the holes in the ground. Grab the point spheres along the way, and Force Push the mines off the walkway. When you reach the walkway's end, drop down the long shaft to the corridor below.

Droid-jack the chameleon droid in the corridor, and use it to blow open the grate at the end of the corridor. Pass through the grate and enter a large area with jets of steam hissing to your left and right. The steam on the left is constant, but the jet on the right periodically stops. Turn right and wait for the steam jets to die down, then double-jump over the jets.

Return to the area right of the platform—where the console is—but this time proceed past the console. Step on the next giant piston and launch yourself across the gap on the right, over two sabotage droids. Take out the droids on the other side of the gap, then use one of the nearby pistons to leap onto the next platform on the right.

Step onto the giant piston on the ground and jump right, onto the large platform.

From the platform, either piston-jump across the next right gap or use the small platform along the far wall to carefully climb down onto the next area.

Jump back down onto the other side of the platform and collect the point spheres above the two large pistons. Destroy the chameleon droids in the immediate vicinity, then walk up to the computer console in the top right and stick your lightsaber through it. This destroys the console and deactivates the steam jets on the left of the area where you started. After destroying the console, you can optionally return to the starting area and collect the point spheres and point crystals left of the now-deactivated steam jets; however, this does not gain you many points.

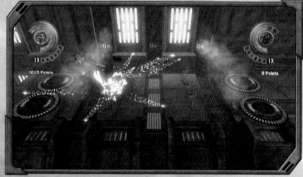

Wait for the steam jets to dissipate, then jump over them into a new section of the walkway. When you do, several battle droids attack from both sides. Stay near the middle and use Force Blasts and lightsaber combos to take them all out. After taking them out, leap over the next steam jets toward an area with four giant pistons.

Alternatively, you can use a piston to jump and grab an Invincibility power-up. Landing in the steam won't hurt you, and lightsaber throws and Force Blasts should be all that's necessary to progress.

When you reach the area with the four giant pistons, you can take part in a Point Panic challenge.

In the Wii and PSP versions, steam does not come out of the vents, and there is no mission challenge in the PSP version.

Leave the area and climb atop the long pipe on the far right. Follow it out to the right, grabbing the point spheres along the way. When you reach the bend in the pipe, jump onto the next pipe—the one on the left—then follow the second pipe left.

Follow the pipe to the next area and immediately jack the chameleon droid and maneuver it over the square grating near the center. Drop a mine over the grate and blow it up! Once it's gone, drop through the hole in the ground.

ARTIFACT

An artifact is inside a tall shaft attached to the second pipe. Immediately after jumping onto it, bound back and forth, up the walls until you reach the artifact. If you don't want to wall-bound up, you can also follow the pipe out and around to a series of poles you can use to swing up to the artifact.

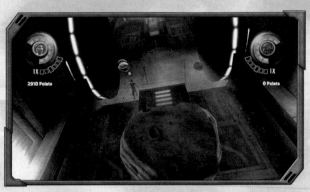

You drop down into a large asteroid-smashing tunnel. Hop off the asteroid and approach the mashing pistons on the left and right. Quickly jump onto the small floating rock, then jump across the gap to the other side.

Be sure to grab all of the point spheres lining the sides of the tunnel as you go.

In the Wii and PSP versions, there are no rocks, just maintenance droids.

When you reach the next two asteroid mashers, jump atop the sabotage droid, then double-jump across the next few asteroid pieces to a square platform. Use the Force to open the hatch on the left and step onto the elevator on the other side.

In the Wii and PSP versions, there is no sabotage droid; there are only maintenance droids. In addition, you open a door, not a hatch.

The elevator takes you to the communications tower where you find a mysterious Skakoan. Before you can arrest him, however, he zips away!

Abandon Ship! Juma-9-Mission 5

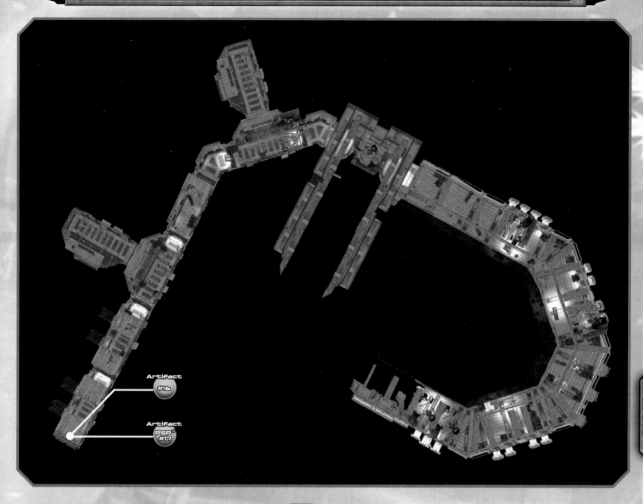

Artifact
#16

Artifact
PSP
#17

As Master Kenobi sets off after the mysterious Skakoan, he orders his men to evacuate the entire space station. Despite having just secured cargo decks one and two, the clone troopers must now shift their attention to the evacuation instead.

NOTE

During this mission, you take control of the clone trooper Switch.

Even the Brave Must Run Sometimes

ARTIFACT

You can find an artifact behind this level's starting location.

Pass through the first gate ahead and immediately take cover behind the small crates in the corridor. Open fire on the super battle droids as they march out of the side corridor. Hold your position there until all the super battle droids stop attacking. If any of the droids get too close for comfort, knock them back with melee attacks, then take them out. You can also kneel behind the boxes and continuously fire through the door. This should fend most of them off, and your allies can clean up any that get through.

PRIMAGAMES.COM

Enter the next section of the corridor, and rush behind the crates on the right. Take aim at the hatch on the left and wait for more droids to come marching out. Lob some electro-grenades at them as they approach, then finish them off with blaster fire.

Dash across the holo-bridge into the next part of the station. Rush down the ramp on the other side and blast the battle droids waiting to ambush you. Toss a few grenades if you need to. Once the area is clear, approach the console along the far left wall. As you do so, more droids will appear, so be prepared!

Trash the droid soldiers, and rush up the ramp ahead. Follow it to another small section of the corridor where a squad of droids attacks. Grab the explosive grenades from the station on the right, then chuck some grenades at the attacking battle droids. After taking out the first wave, a second wave marches in from the left. Blow them up, then do an about-face in the corridor. Try to keep at least one thermal detonator in your inventory for the next group of droids you encounter.

Hack the computer console to activate the first batch of escape pods. Cover your men as they escape, then grab the rocket launcher upgrades on the right.

A pair of gold droideka roll in from behind. Throw a grenade at them and disrupt their shields. Once their shields are down, throw another grenade and obliterate them. Turn back around, grab some more grenades, then proceed down the corridor.

PSP-NOTES
In the PSP version, rotate the outer ring to the left once, the middle ring to the right once, and the inner ring to the right twice.

Run right, to the next section, and confront the batch of droids. Hit the droideka first with a rocket, then blast the other droids to bits before hacking the next console.

PSP-NOTES
There are no gold droideka in the PSP version.

HACK!
This console is a bit tricky. First move the smallest, inner ring section right so that it faces the bottom left. Rotate the medium-sized ring section so it faces the top right, then do the same with the third green ring section. Once the first, second, and third ring sections are in place, return to the smallest ring and rotate it left into place.

66

-Pack in there!

Load up on grenades as you approach the next section, then vault over the crates in your way. Skip over the next two rows of crates until you reach another clone battalion battling it out against a battle droid squad. Help your men obliterate the enemy with a few grenades, then hack the third console.

HACK!

To hack this console, rotate the second ring left until the green section faces the bottom right. Switch to the inner ring and rotate it left until the blue ring faces to the lower left. Next, switch back to the second ring and rotate it right one more time until the blue and green ring sections line up.

NOTE

There is a Droid Demolition challenge in between the two rows of crates.

PSP NOTES

In the PSP version, slice the console by rotating the outer ring to the right twice, rotating the inner ring to the left twice, and moving the outer ring into place. Also, there is no mission challenge in this location.

After hacking the third console, another batch of your men get to escape through the pods. Continue moving right along the walkway until you reach the final batch of escape pods. When you do, your men slip in and prepare to launch the pods into space. Unfortunately, the pods won't activate from the inside.

That's when one brave soldier, Switch, exits his pod to activate the other pods from the outside. As time runs out, Switch closes the hatches to all of the pods and stays behind to make sure they launch. He sacrifices himself in order for the rest of the men to escape....

67

My Name Is Kul Teska: Juma-9-Mission 6

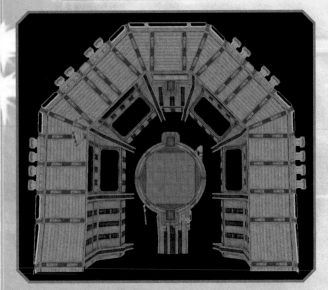

Two versus One. Yours, the Advantage Is

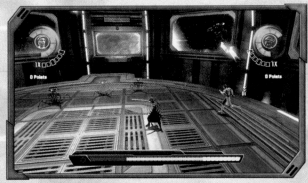

Kul Teska immediately opens fire, takes flight, and begins roaming around the outer edge of the arena. As he speeds around the outer edge like a coward, several chameleon droids appear on your platform and drop mines.

> There is no escape, Skakoan.

> You can't bargain without bringing something to the table.

When Obi-Wan and Plo Koon finally catch up to the Skakoan, they trap him in a small section of the ship.

He tries to bargain for the lives of the clones at first, but when neither Jedi Master gives in, he threatens to blow up all of the escape pods that just left the station!

Just as the Skakoan is about to press the button on his detonator, Obi-Wan Force Pushes the device out of his hand. Of course, that won't stop the Skakoan; it'll only slow him down.

Wait for the droids to drop their mines, then stand near the center of the platform. When Kul zooms by along the outer edge, use a Force Push to slam the mines into the flying pest. The explosion disrupts his boosters, and he comes crashing down onto your platform.

Once he's down, rush the Skakoan and unleash a flurry of lightsaber combos. He eventually gets back into the air and begins attacking using a grappling hook. As soon as his grappling hook lands on the platform, double-jump away and dodge his slam attack. He'll also use his blaster against you, which can be blocked with lightsaber blocks.

NOTE

You control Obi-Wan during this fierce battle.

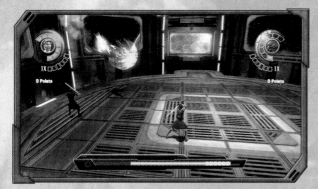

Continue dashing around the arena until he begins using a swooping cannonball attack. Simply dash out of the way or lightsaber block when he charges up, and wait for him to stop his cannonball attacks.

Knock down Kul again by launching the mines into him, then slash at him again to dwindle his Health bar. Repeat this process again until he decides to change tactics.

After losing nearly half his health, Kul Teska begins to tear apart the platform. Dodge the piece of platform he throws at you, then run to the center of the arena. When Kul begins to fire his laser beam at you, move out of the way slightly or block with your lightsaber, then creep out to the edge near where Kul is floating.

Use Force Blasts to bounce back the rockets he shoots at you and send him crashing down onto the platform. While he's down, slash at him with your lightsaber and chop off more of his health. Repeat the process again until he flees to the small window at the arena's far end.

From there, Kul will begin to hurl crates at you. As the crates rise from the gap in front of you, wait for them get within Force Pushing distance and slam them into Teska. If he manages to grab them with his grappling hook and hurls them at you, be sure to block them. Hurl crates back at him when he stands and taunts you to defeat the cowardly Skakoan!

After taking enough damage, the window behind Kul Teska shatters and he is blown out into space! Of course, that doesn't mean that he will die. He's protected by his suit, and he simply zooms away. Chances are he'll be back again....

In the meantime, you're trapped in the small space station room!

ACT 2

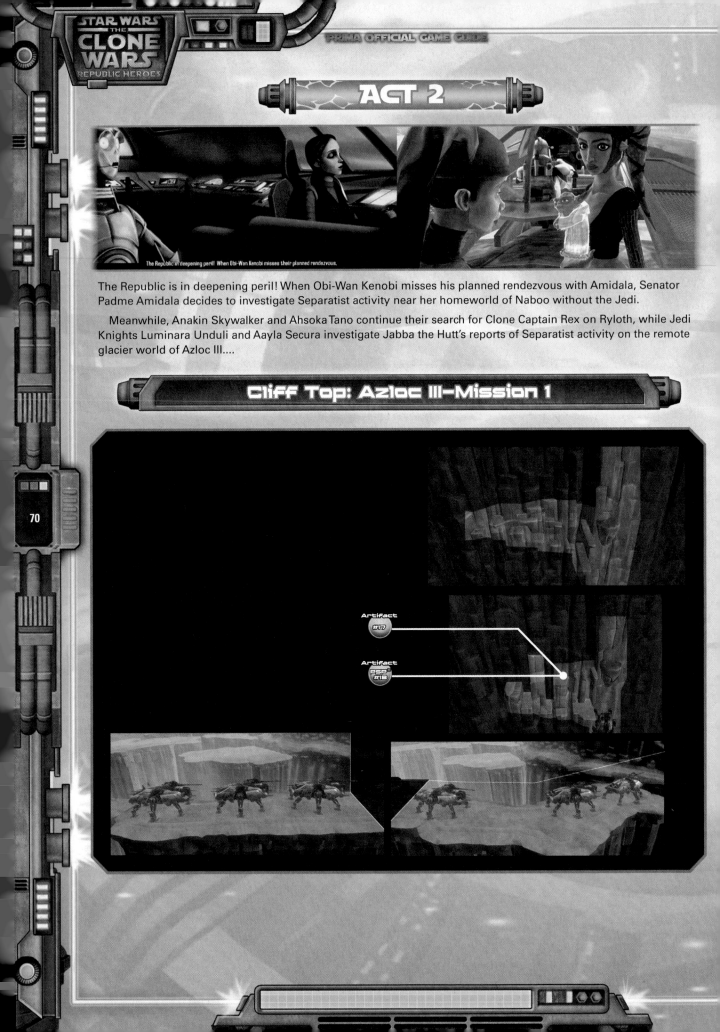

The Republic in deepening peril! When Obi-Wan Kenobi misses their planned rendezvous.

The Republic is in deepening peril! When Obi-Wan Kenobi misses his planned rendezvous with Amidala, Senator Padme Amidala decides to investigate Separatist activity near her homeworld of Naboo without the Jedi.

Meanwhile, Anakin Skywalker and Ahsoka Tano continue their search for Clone Captain Rex on Ryloth, while Jedi Knights Luminara Unduli and Aayla Secura investigate Jabba the Hutt's reports of Separatist activity on the remote glacier world of Azloc III....

Cliff Top: Azloc III–Mission 1

Artifact
#17

Artifact
PSP
#18

As Jedi Knights Luminara Unduli and Aayla Secura ride toward the coordinates provided by Jabba the Hutt, they express their concerns to Master Yoda about trusting the greedy Hutt. Master Yoda sets their concerns at ease and urges the duo to proceed with their mission, however uncertain they may be.

As their transport vehicle slowly stomps toward the coordinates, they sense something big, something disturbing....

NOTE

During this mission, you play as Aayla Secura.

Trust Not in Jabba, Trust in Jabba's Greed, You Must

As the transport vehicle nears the glacial cliffs ahead, jump on top of your vehicle's gun turret and slink out to its end. From the turret, double-jump onto the back of the next vehicle. Continue moving up the vehicles until you reach the one at the front of the line.

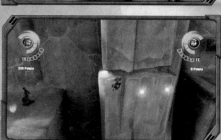

When the vehicles reach the cliff side, the clones prepare to march them up it. Unfortunately, the vehicles' path is blocked by an outcropping of ice. If they blasted it, they would risk bringing down the whole cliff side on top of themselves. Jump onto the small ledge on the left and follow the cliff side to a tall, shaftlike opening.

Step inside the shaft and bounce back and forth up the walls until you reach the ledge on the left. Break the point crystal on it, then leap out over the shaft to grab a hold of the thin ledge carved into the tall rock on the right. Run right to the other side of the rock, then launch yourself onto the next small ledge.

PSP NOTES

In the PSP version, there's no point crystal.

ARTIFACT

An artifact is located just above this small ledge. To reach it, jump onto the platform on the right, then leap left onto the ledge with the artifact!

Jump across the ledges on the right until you reach a ledge blocked by the ice outcropping.

To destroy the ice outcropping, double-jump onto the nearby sabotage droid and charge it. Aim the charged droid toward the outcropping and let it fly. When the droid collides with the ice, it shatters it into a million harmless little pieces.

71

With the outcropping out of the way, the transport vehicle is able to climb up the cliff. Jump back onto the vehicle and ride it up the cliff side. When it stops near the next ledge, hop onto it.

Just as before, follow the ledges as they lead left across the cliff until you come across another small ledge carved into the rock face. Leap out and grab it, then follow the ledge around the rock to a tall shaft. Bounce back and forth up the wall until you reach the next ledge on the left.

Grab the small ridge and wall-run around to the tall rock's other side. Leap onto the ledge on the right, and follow it down to another large rock blocking your path.

> **NOTE**
>
> There is a Droid Demolition challenge at the end of the small icy bridge.

Wait for a sabotage droid to decloak, then double-jump onto it immediately. Charge the droid and launch it at the rock blocking your path. When the rock explodes, the transport vehicle marches up the side of the cliff and pulls up next to your platform.

From here, jump out to the next ridge along the pillar on the left and grab it. Follow it around to the pillar's left side. You can't hoist yourself up onto the pillar yet, so jump off the pillar onto the ledge on the left.

Double-jump right onto the pillar and dash up the long icy bridge on the right. Follow the bridge to a small platform, then jump down onto the ledge on the bridge's other side. Carefully approach the next edge of the platform and launch yourself at the tall rock on your right.

Once again, leap back onto the transport vehicle and ride it to the top of the cliff. When you reach the top, you can see over to the other side of the cliffs. From there, you spy a large, unnatural crater. At first glance it looks like a simple crash site. But after more careful observation, you see that much of the wreckage is floating over the crash site. Without a closer look, there's no telling what could have caused such a strange phenomenon....

Ground Zero: Azloc III-Mission 2

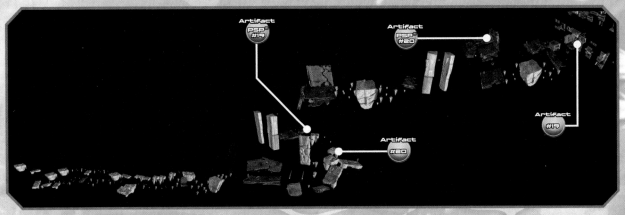

Upon reaching the top of the cliffs, you clearly see the damage from the demolished ship. The floating debris forms small, precarious pathways across the crash site. Before you set out across the ice shards, a small troop of clone soldiers zooms away ahead of you on their jetpacks.

A Careful Step, a Jedi Must Always Take

Carefully traipse right, across the large ice platform to several smaller ice shards floating just off in the distance. Hop across the small ice shard toward the long, pole-shaped beams and either swing across them or hop along the small shards next to them.

When you reach the next large platform, creep out to the edge and jump onto the small ice shard nearby. Carefully dance across the next series of ice shards until you reach a platform with a point crystal on it. Shatter the crystal, then swing off the ledge onto the next series of small floating shards.

When you reach the L-shaped platform, hold your position long enough for your men to blow up some more ice ahead of you. The debris from their explosion creates more small ice platforms to hop across.

PSP NOTES

In the PSP version, there is already a platform you can use to cross this area.

Bounce from shard to shard, collecting point spheres as you go. Land on either of the two long platforms ahead. The left platform has a checkpoint, but the right platform leads to the next section. If you activate the checkpoint on the left platform, hop across the small ice chunk floating between them and land on the right platform.

Swing from the right platform onto the large ice chunk ahead, and stop when you reach a tall icy rock surrounded by several point spheres. Leap out onto the tall rock and grab the thin ledge etched into it. Run around the rock, collecting the points as you go, then spring onto the long platform on the other side.

NOTE

If you land on the right platform, take part in the Point Panic challenge.

ARTIFACT

An artifact is located on a small ice rock just below and left of the tall rock surrounded by point spheres. Grab it just before you jump onto the tall rock.

PSP AND WII NOTES

In the Wii and PSP versions, the tall rock is not present and the artifact is at the top of the first wall in the wall-jump puzzle. In the PSP version, there is no mission challenge in this location.

Break the point crystal on this platform, then turn left. Follow the small icy shards to another small, square platform. Follow the debris left as it rises higher into the air until you reach another floating piece of debris with a point crystal on it.

Double-jump onto the next large ice chunk on the right and grab on to the thin ledge carved into it. Run around the rock to its other side, then carefully wall-jump back and forth until you reach the top. Climb atop the left side of the tall rock, then jump onto the thick piece of debris on the right. Follow it right to the second piece of debris, then jump onto the large, square piece of metal on the left.

Wait for two spider droids to pop up, then droid-jack one of them. Aim at the large stone ahead and blast it to pieces! While you do, Luminara destroys the second spider droid.

NOTE

After shattering the rock in your way, a Knockback Knockout challenge appears on this platform. See the "Knockback Knockout Tips" section in the Ways of the Force chapter for tips on how to beat it.

PSP AND WII NOTES

In the Wii and PSP versions, there's no mission challenge in this location.

The shattered rock creates a series of ice platforms leading deeper into the crash site. Hop across them until you reach another large floating rock with several point spheres surrounding it. Grab on to it, follow it around, then wall-jump all the way up.

PSP AND WII NOTES

In the Wii and PSP versions, an artifact is in the middle of a platform after the second wall-jump puzzle.

Turn right at the top and follow the debris to a series of large platforms. Make a right at the platforms and crush the few sabotage droids that attack. When the spider droids join the fight, droid-jack one of them and aim its blaster turret at the large chunk of ice in the distance.

Blow it to smithereens, then rush across the platforms to the corner of the floating debris. As you land, use either a super jump attack or Force Blast to demolish the battle droids on the piece of floating metal, then make a left across the newly formed path of ice shards.

PSP AND WII NOTES

In the Wii and PSP versions, there is no ice chunk to destroy.

When you reach the long platform, turn left and unleash a Force Blast on the battle droids perched on the platform above and to your left. Knock them off their perch and destroy them.

Turn right, then jump across several more pieces of floating debris. Follow it left, then go right toward the large destroyed structure.

ARTIFACT

Just before the debris path turns left and sweeps back around, there is an artifact floating above one of the small chunks of demolished ship. Grab it as you go.

When you reach the entrance to the demolished ship, you find nothing but scrap metal. Still, from a distance you can sense something sinister, something dark....

PSP AND WII NOTES

In the PSP version, the ship won't be present. Just follow the path until it ends.

STAR WARS
THE
CLONE
WARS
REPUBLIC HEROES

PRIMA OFFICIAL GAME GUIDE

Take It Back: Juma-9-Mission 7

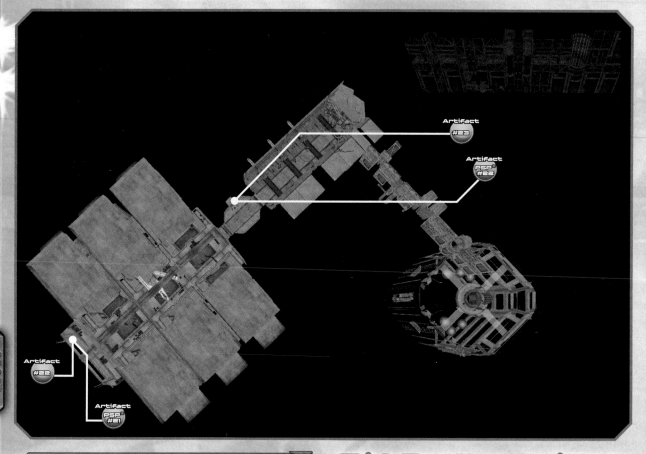

Artifact #23

Artifact PSP #22

Artifact #22

Artifact PSP #21

76

Elsewhere in the galaxy, a small drop ship pulls into the Juma-9 space station and drops off Jedi Knights Mace Windu and Kit Fisto. Upon arriving, they receive a report from the clone soldiers rescued from the escape pods. They say that Generals Kenobi and Koon are still somewhere in the station.

NOTE

During this mission, you take control of Mace Windu.

Stick Together, Jedi Must

To begin a thorough search for the two lost Jedi Knights, first familiarize yourself with the station's layout. From the landing area, turn right and dash across the hangar bay, blasting the first row of battle droids with the Force.

ARTIFACT

An artifact is located high atop a crate in the corner of the hangar bay, near where you land. To reach it, climb atop the crates to the right, then double-jump left onto the crates and grab it before continuing deeper into the station.

PSP AND WII NOTES

In the Wii and PSP versions, the artifact is behind the crates on the ground.

Turn left and locate the three super battle droids that emerge from the elevator lift on the side. Droid-jack one of them and use it against the other droids in the immediate area. Proceed right, toward the next small droid group, and lunge into their ranks. Wait for several sabotage droids to appear; either jack them and use them as weapons or crush them with jump attacks.

After destroying the sabotage droids, turn to the chameleon droids and crush them. Once the area is clear, move right again until you encounter more resistance.

TIP

There are tons of point spheres scattered around the landing area. Pick them all up as you fight. Not only will you rack up the points, but you'll also make full use of the wide-open area as you battle the dozens of droids.

PSP AND WII NOTES

In the Wii and PSP versions, there are no sabotage or chameleon droids in this area.

Grab the red power-up atop the crates on the left, then rush the droids on the other side of the small crates. Force Push the crates into the droids, then sweep the area with lightsaber combos to finish them all off.

Storm down the landing bay until you reach the end, where several more droids await. Droid-jack a super battle droid and use it to thin the droids' numbers. After taking out as many as you can with the super battle droid, hop off and use a jump attack to demolish several more metal pests.

NOTE

After clearing the area of all enemies, two challenges appear nearby. The challenge on the right is a Takeover Takedown; the one on the right is Droid Demolition.

PSP AND WII NOTES

In the Wii version, Takeover Takedown is the only available mission challenge. In the PSP version, there is no mission challenge.

Pass through the hangar bay doors into the station, and rush the sabotage droids in the next chamber. Take on one while Kit Fisto takes on the other.

PSP NOTES

In the PSP version, you'll face super battle droids here instead.

77

ARTIFACT

There's another artifact in this section. After destroying the droids, break open the crates along the back wall to find it!

PSP AND WII NOTES

In the Wii and PSP versions, the artifact is located behind a grate on the back wall.

Pass through the hatch into the next area, where several more droids are stationed. There, lining the long, winding corridor, are several giant cannons firing on the planet below. Dash past the first cannon and pounce on the nearest super battle droid. Jack the clanker and turn it on the others in the room.

Fight past the next few groups of droids, jacking super battle droids and crushing other droids with jump attacks until you reach the corridor's end. Grab the red power-up in the corner and follow the fallen twisted beam up toward the burning wreckage overhead.

Jump from the beam onto the long twisted pipe above you. Climb the pipe onto the burning wreckage. Make a right, and enter the next area of the station.

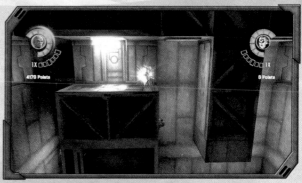

Hop across the small gap ahead, then launch yourself at the wall ahead of you. Use your lightsaber to slide down, and jump backward onto the wall behind you to slide down some more. Just before you fall into the pit below, leap backward onto the next corridor.

Wall-jump up the shaft at the corridor's end, then lightsaber-slide down the next wall just as you did before. This time, however, when you launch yourself off the second wall, grab the poles nearby and swing across them to another tall shaft area. Wall-bound up to the next corridor, and hop down the long circular shaft at the end.

The shaft leads to a large, circular platform with a hole in the center. Kill the battle droid here. Before long, a magna guard pops up from the center of the platform. Droid-jack the magna guard and crush him from above.

Return to the center of the platform and wait for the third wave of enemies to come pouring in. This time, three small battalions of battle droids emerge from three circular platforms. Grab the red power-up on the platform and dash around the area, destroying droids as you go.

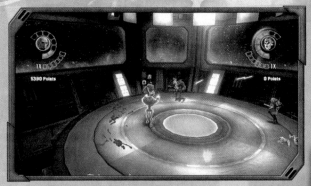

As soon as you destroy the magna guard, two red holo-bridges activate from the surrounding outer ring, and more droids come storming out of the hatches. Blast them with the Force as they approach, and knock them off the bridges before they can reach you.

If any of the droids reach the platform, run your lightsaber through them and dispatch them quickly. After you destroy the first wave of droids, several sabotage droids decloak directly above you. Double-jump into the air and come down on them with your lightsaber, crushing the floating droids into a dazzling display of flying parts.

Watch for more super battle droids to pop up, and crush them quickly.

NOTE
A Droid Demolition challenge appears after enduring all of the droid waves.

PSP NOTES
In the PSP version, there are no sabotage droids present.

After destroying all the droids, the final platform rises nearby, and a blue holo-bridge connects both areas. Cross the bridge and take the new platform to the another part of the station. The station is still in a state of disarray. It's up to you and the clones to repair it!

Inside Out: Juma-9-Mission 8

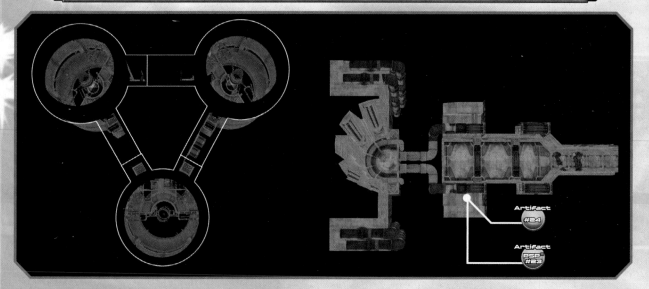

Elsewhere on the space station, a small troop of clone soldiers tramples across the station's surface toward its capacitor. In order to bring the core back online, however, the capacitor chain must be operational. While the clones go about their mission, the other two Jedi head to the core reactor.

NOTE

During this mission, you take control of a clone trooper.

Do Your Part while Others Do Theirs

Storm up the corridor and use your jetpack to boost over the pits blocking your path. When you land on the other side, quickly blast the puny battle droids. Strafe around the crab droids and shoot them so they block, making themselves vulnerable from the back.

PSP NOTES

In the PSP version, you'll battle sabotage droids instead of crab droids.

Stay on the area's outer edge, picking off the droids as they attack. After clearing the area, hack both of the consoles along the walls to disable the electrical field blocking your path.

HACK!

The console on the left doesn't have any red ring sections, so it's very easy to hack: simply shift all of the ring sections into place. To hack the console on the right, rotate the innermost ring to the top left. Rotate the second ring left so it locks into place, with the green ring section facing the upper left. Finally, rotate the inner ring right until the blue ring sections line up.

PSP NOTES

In the PSP version, the console on the left has only one red section, so it won't interfere with you as you line up the green parts. The one on the right has just one green part.

Jetpack over the large coil ahead of you into the second area. Stop before you are fried by the next electrified coil. Several crab droids drop in. Destroy them, then immediately get to work on the consoles and hack them.

HACK!

Hack the left console by rotating the third ring right twice, so the green section faces the lower right. Rotate the second ring once to the right, so the green sections all line up. Finally, rotate the smallest blue ring left until all blue ring sections line up. The console on the right is another simple hack; simply line them all up.

PSP NOTES

In the PSP version, both consoles have just one green segment.

NOTE

After hacking both consoles, a Droid Demolition challenge appears.

Float over the next coil after hacking both consoles and deactivating the electrical field. Stop in the next section before heading directly into more electrified coils. Boost up to the crates on the left. Use your blaster to shoot at the vulture droid on the other side while dodging its attack.

Let the other clone soldiers handle the droids across the gap while you focus solely on the vulture droid. Continue blasting at it while moving from side to side, dodging its fire whenever possible.

ARTIFACT

An artifact is located directly behind the rocket-launcher station on the left. Grab it while you battle the vulture droid!

Once the vulture droid falls, cross the two coils bridging the gap to where the vulture droid was perched, and hack the two consoles in that area.

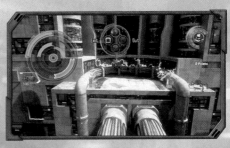

HACK!

To hack the console on the left, rotate the second ring left until it lines up with the first ring. Then rotate the fourth ring left once to lock them all in place. The console on the right is even easier to hack—rotate the third ring right, until it's in place, then move the second ring right until it is also in place.

Once you've successfully hacked both consoles, you bring the capacitors back online. After passing along the good news to Generals Windu and Fisto, they take over.

NOTE

You've done your job, soldier. It's time to take control of Mace Windu from here.

Immediately after taking control of Jedi Master Windu, use the Force to shove the cylinders into the walls. However, in order to get things up and running, you must insert the cylinders in order. In this room, place them in order from left to right (one, two, and three, with two being the center cylinder).

If you insert them out of order, you'll get a prompt from Maser Yoda on how to place them back in place. Once the cylinders are in place, the large electrical field at the center of the area comes back online and the doors open, leading to another reactor core generator.

TIP

You only need to use the Force on each cylinder once. Your companions will do the rest on each one. Also, this puzzle is timed, and the cylinders will eventually pop out if you take too long.

Jump across the moving platforms in the corridor and enter the next reactor core area. This time, place the cylinders in the following order: center, left, then right (two, one, three).

Enter the next room and insert the final cylinders in the following order: left, right, then center (one, three, two).

Once you've brought all three reactor core generators back online, communications is restored! Just then, the two Jedi receive an incoming transmission from a clone elsewhere on the station.

It's Switch! He survived the explosion after the escape pods ejected! He insists that he can find the two missing generals, Plo and Kenobi, but he'll need time first to recalibrate the internal sensors....

82

Eye of the Storm: Azloc III-Mission 3

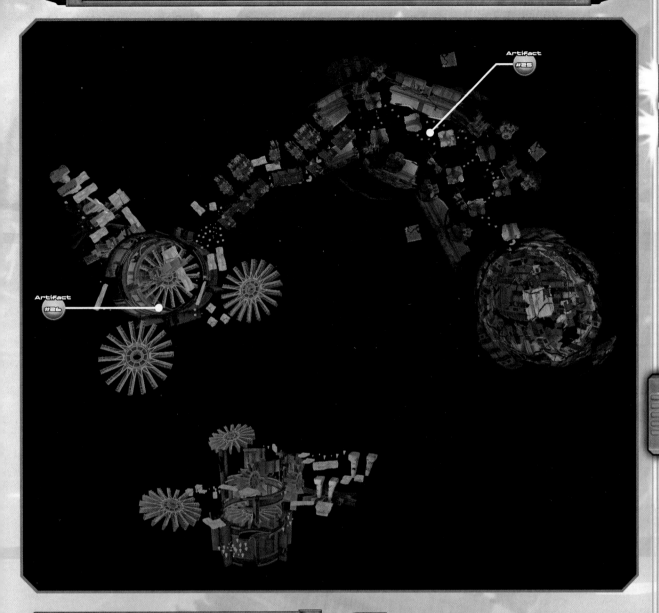

Artifact
#25

Artifact
#26

This looks like the point of origin.

NOTE

You take control of Jedi Knight Luminara during this mission.

PSP NOTES

You don't play this section in the PSP version. Skip to Guard Duty: Alzoc III—Mission 4.

Back on Azloc III, the clone troopers rendezvous with Luminara and Aayla. As the group nears the point of origin in the crash site, a vulture droid zooms in and lands almost directly on top of them!

Light the Way, Luminara Must

The vulture droid is the largest droid you've faced yet. As soon as it lands and begins to stomp around the area, let Aayla lock down one of the droid's legs with the Force. As soon as she has it held, lash out at it with your lightsaber and bring the vulture droid crashing down on its body. You'll have to do this twice, and you may need to use the Force on the droid yourself.

As soon as the droid is down, climb up one of its legs onto its head and stab it with your lightsaber. Once you've destroyed it, set out to find the ship's data recorder. It'll be the best way to find out what happened.

Hop across the debris on the right toward the next red force field, and either Force Blast the battle droids in your way, or knock their rockets back at them as you go. Follow the floating debris around, past more droids, until you reach the final platform, just right of the next shield generator.

Demolish the droids on the platform until the sabotage droids decloak. When they do, jack one of them and hurl it at the shield generator to drop the red force field on the right.

Jump right onto a floating piece of debris, then double-jump onto the next platform. Sprint right, past the large doorway, into the next area. As you enter, a large shield generator explodes and the red force field disappears.

Return to the platform on the far right, then turn left, past the now-deactivated force field. Destroy the four battle droids on the second piece of large debris. Continue hopping across small pieces of debris until you reach a large platform floating next to a large red force field.

ARTIFACT

An artifact is floating amidst the debris between large platforms here. To grab it, follow the path of debris on the left between platforms.

Once again, wait for the sabotage droids to appear, and jack one of them to use as an explosive on the nearby shield generator. Do an about-face and jump across more debris toward the next shield generator. Destroy this one just as you did the others—with a sabotage droid—and bring down the next force field.

Dash past the new fallen force field and into a new area full of droids. This time, destroy all the spider droids and wait for a sabotage droid to appear. When it does, jack it and launch it at the generator deep in the distance.

Jump left, across the fallen force field, and crush the chameleon droids on the next platform. Use jump attacks to destroy them.

Follow the floating planks of debris right, until it sweeps around to a large open area with a big stone blocking the path on the left. Jack the chameleon droid nearby and set a series of mines near the large stone to blow it up.

Leap from ice shard to ice shard to the walkway on the left, and use jump attacks to destroy the droids in your  way. Make a right on the walkway, following it up toward another series of ice chunks. Jump across them, collecting point spheres as you go, until you reach the rim of a large demolished structure.

Follow the rim right, toward the large spinning cog, and jump left onto one of the cog's teeth.

TIP

To collect all of the point spheres around the cog, simply stand in place and ride the cog all the way around.

ARTIFACT

Stay put on the cog's teeth and ride it as it spins around. As you do, you'll collect an artifact!

Ride the cog to the platform on the far left, and hop off before it spins around a second time. Climb up the two ice platforms to a second cog, this one twisted down at an angle, and hop on for another ride. Jump off the cog, onto another series of debris platforms that lead to a third giant cog.

Make a right at the shaft's top, and wall-bound up the next tall gap in the walls. This time, make a left and saunter out to the long ice walkways leading to another round rim. Follow the rim right to the next series of ice platforms.

The third spinning cog is dangerous. Instead of jumping onto it, wait for the large teeth to pass you, then double-jump over it onto the next side of the ice platform. Hop onto the rim on the right and carefully jump out onto the small ice shards ahead of you.

Wait for the next large cog to spin past you, then double-jump from the small ice shard onto the long thin walkway across from you. Make a left at the walkway's end, and wall-bound up the tall shaft to the next area.

Follow the path as it wends left, to another large spinning cog. Hop on and ride it to the top left door. Jump off to reach your destination. Open the door for your clone soldiers and send them inside to find the ship's data recorder!

CAUTION

Stay off the third and fourth cogs. Don't try to jump onto them or bounce off them to reach the next area. If you touch them, you'll die!

Guard Duty: Azloc III—Mission 4

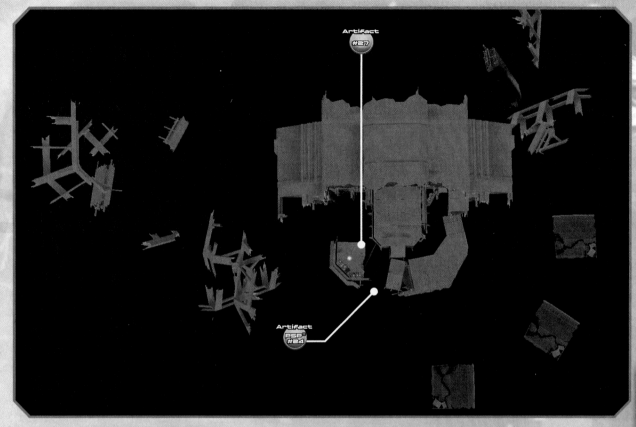

87

On the door's other side is the ship's main computer. While the clone soldiers slice into it, you'll cover their back and keep those pesky droids from interfering with them.

Surrounded on All Sides, You Will Be

As soon as Commander Gree gets to work on slicing into the ship's computer, a whole swarm of droids attacks!

Battle droids march in from the hatch behind you while spider droids call up from the side of the platform. When the spider droid reaches you, blast it with the Force and knock it off, leaving the battle droids behind you.

PSP NOTES

In the PSP version, there are no spider droids present.

Dash into their ranks and slice through them with your lightsaber. When the jetpack-toting battle droids zoom in, hit them with a Force Blast and finish them off with a few lightsaber combos. Use Lightsaber Throws, Force Kills, and Force Blasts on the battle droids, and use jump attacks on the super battle droids.

Leave Aayla to handle any leftover battle droids while you take on the spider droid that climbs up the side of the platform. When the super battle droids storm out of the hatch, leap onto the long, half-circle platform on the right. Eliminate the new battle droids first.

An artifact is located on the corner of the platform with the main computer. Grab it during battle.

PSP AND WII NOTES

In the Wii and PSP versions, the artifact is on a platform that is to the bottom left of the starting area.

After clearing out the long walkway, return to the main platform where the super battle droids attack your men. Either jack one of the super battle droids and blast the others to bits, or use jump attacks to slash them all at once. When the next wave of droids rushes in, they bring crab droids along for the fight.

Double-jump onto one of the crab droids on the long platform, then jump off onto the high ledge above you. Grab the red power-up and hop back down to the main platform below. Droid-jack the nearest crab droid and turn it on the other droids in the area.

PSP AND WII NOTES

In the Wii and PSP versions, there is a console on the top ledge and no power-up. You'll need to slice it to move on. The power-up is on a platform at the bottom right of the level.

After fending off the crab droids, a pair of droideka roll in from the hatch. Greet them with a Force Blast to disable their shields, then pounce on them with a jump attack. Take out the droideka, then turn on the sabotage droids near the computer platform. Jack them and send them crashing into each other to destroy them.

NOTE

After dispatching the sabotage droids, a Droid Demolition challenge and a Takeover Takedown challenge appear.

PSP NOTES

In the PSP version, there are no droideka present, and only the Droid Demolition challenge is available.

After covering your men's hide, Commander Gree is able to slice into the ship's main computer. Join him on the computer deck to learn what he found out. The ship's holo-recorder shows a smaller ship docking with a ship only minutes before the other ship crashed!

After the mysterious small ship departs, the large ship explodes! When you access the crashed ship's manifest, you find it was carrying two strange crates—one of them is now missing.

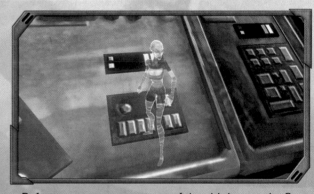

Before you can access more of the ship's records, Gree finds one more recent entry. It's Asajj Ventress, and she's activated the self-destruct mode in what remains of the crashed vessel!

It's a Trap! Alzoc III—Mission 5

WALKTHROUGH

It's a Trap! Alzoc III—Mission 5

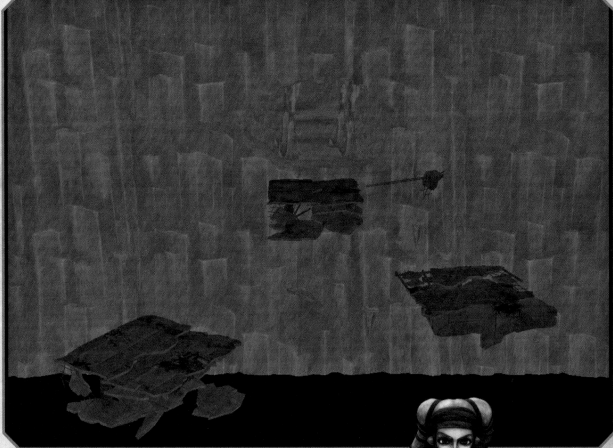

Luminara, Aayla, and their clones speed off just in time to avoid being caught in the ship's blast. Though they escape the ship's blast, they fall at the feet of their worst nightmare—Asajj Ventress!

 NOTE

During this trial, you take control of Aayla Secura. Good luck!

A True Test, the Dark One Is

After a bit of banter, Ventress draws her lightsabers and attacks! Hit her with lightsaber combos and begin wearing her down.

Stay near the center of the first platform and back away when Ventress crosses her lightsabers behind her back to block. Resume your attack only after you have a clean shot for solid blows.

This time, after taking even more damage (when you've depleted all of the orange in her Health bar), Ventress flees to the cave near the far wall of the cliffs. Follow her again and stay on the platform floating just off the cave entrance. If you try to reach the cave, you'll fall down the cliff side.

From your platform, fend off the sabotage droids that appear and dodge or block Ventress's attacks. When the spider droids appear, jack one of them or a sabotage droid, and blast the four pillars supporting the cave over Ventress's head.

When Ventress takes too much damage (as evidenced when all of the yellow in her Health bar is gone), she flees like a coward to another nearby platform. Swing across the floating beams and follow her. Resume your attack just as before.

PSP AND WII NOTES

In the Wii and PSP versions, Ventress jumps to the middle platform after taking a certain amount of damage. When she does this, two sabotage droids will appear. Droid-jack them into Ventress. After this, she'll jump back to the platform to repeat the process.

PSP AND WII NOTES

Like before, in the Wii and PSP versions, Ventress will jump to the middle platform after being hit a certain number of times. When she does this, two sabotage droids will once again appear, which you should droid-jack into Ventress. Repeat this process until her health is in the red.

The cave collapses over Asajj Ventress's head, burying the Sith in icy rubble. Now, if only you could untangle this web. What does the strange gravity weapon—the missing cargo—have to do with Dooku and his Separatist forces? And who has the stolen weapon?

Enemies of My Enemies: Ryloth-Mission 9

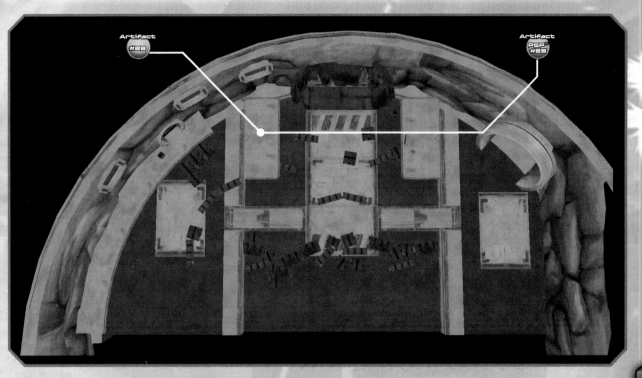

Back on Ryloth, a man in a big hat holds two clone troopers hostage. His name is Cad Bane, and he's in possession of the stolen crate from the crashed vessel on Azloc III. He threatens to kill the two troopers if they don't do as he says.

As he holds his pistol over the troopers' heads, a squad of battle droids busts in through the wall behind him! With both the Separatists and the Republic after him, he's got no choice but to force the clone soldiers to cooperate with him and save his precious cargo!

NOTE

During this mission, you play as a clone trooper.

Cooperate When Needed to Save Your Own Life

Use the rocket launcher to destroy the wave of droids that pours in on you from the large tunnel on the other side of the area.

Grab the gun power-up over the crates on the right and open fire on the droids as they come in from the center of the bay. Use the large gun to shred the incoming droids, then carefully cut across the bay toward the computer console in the top right corner, directly underneath Cad Bane.

91

Hack the computer console on the right to drop a hatch over the hole where the droids march in. The hatch stops the flow of incoming droids. When it does, finish wiping out the few that remain, then reload on powered-up ammo from the power-up station on the left.

ARTIFACT

An artifact is located directly underneath the overhang on the left, behind some boxes. Grab it before you snag the gun power-up!

HACK!

This computer console is actually very simple to hack. Since there are no red ring sections, all you need to do is rotate the green and blue sections until they line up. The most difficult part of hacking this console is having enough time to do it without being interrupted; therefore, begin the hack when there aren't many droids in the area.

PSP NOTES

In the PSP version, move the outer ring to the left once and the inner ring to the right once.

TIP

If you've saved up enough points, this is an excellent time to purchase the Invulnerability Cheat from the shop. With it active, you can't be interrupted during a hack.

After shutting down the droids' attacks on the main bay, they find two more entryways into the bay from the left! Rush up the ramp on the left and open fire on the droids that march in from the lower left tunnel. Grab some explosive grenades from the crates nearby, then blow up the droids as they come in from the lower left. As soon as they're all gone, rush out to the console near the entrance and hack it to seal it shut!

HACK!

Hack this console by first rotating the third inner ring right so that the green section faces the upper left. Then rotate the second ring right to line up the medium and large sections. Finally, return to the third ring and rotate it right until all of the green sections are lined up!

PSP NOTES

In the PSP version, rotate the outer ring to the left twice so the red is facing the top right; then move the inner ring into place, followed by the outer ring.

When a spider droid crawls out onto the overhang above you, blow it up with a grenade, then restock at the grenade station. Climb up the crates to the second opening and drop another grenade to blow up the approaching droids. As soon as the coast is clear, hack the console on the opening's left.

HACK!

This console is a bit trickier than the other two. Begin by rotating the second ring right so that the green section faces the lower left. Once it's in place, rotate the smaller, inner ring right until it is facing the top right. Finally, rotate the second ring right until all three rings line up.

When the second hatch closes and you defeat the droids, a vulture droid bursts through the first hatch, leaving it a sheet of torn metal. Sprint across the bay, past the vulture droid, while strafing back and forth, firing your blasters.

Take cover behind the crate with the power-up. Aim at the vulture droid and keep blasting. Once you've destroyed it, rush up the ramp on the right to surprise Cad Bade. Before you can reach him, however, a whole new wave of sabotage droids bursts in from the right!

NOTE

After destroying the vulture droid, a Droid Demolition challenge appears near the center of the bay.

Reunion Under Fire: Ryloth-Mission 10

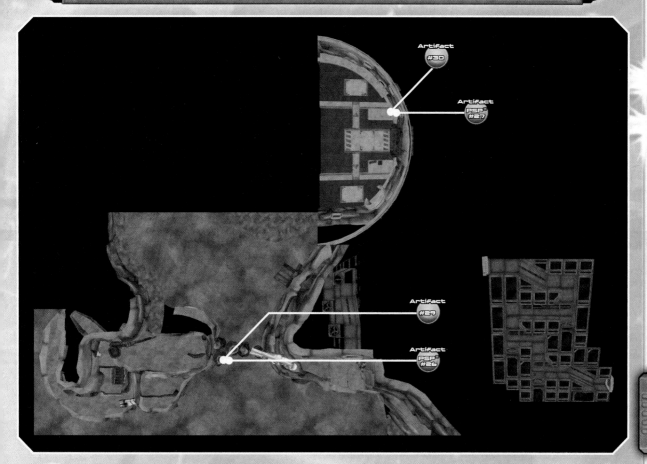

Elsewhere on Ryloth, Anakin Skywalker and Ahsoka Tano search for their missing clone comrades, not knowing they're been kidnapped by Cad Bane! After tuning her senses, Tano is able to locate the missing clone soldier....

NOTE

Ready your lightsaber! You'll be assuming the role of Anakin Skywalker for this rescue mission.

Clear Your Mind, and Find Your Men You Will

Sprint right, around the corner until you run headfirst into a small group of battle droids. Cut them down, then double-jump onto the ledge on the right. Destroy the super battle droid that emerges from the tunnel in the far wall, and double-jump left onto the next platform.

Crush the super battle droid, then turn right and leap onto the area above you. Take out the lone super battle droid in the tall niche, and wall-jump onto the ledge on the right.

PSP NOTES

In the PSP version, the last super battle droid is replaced with three battle droids.

Crush the battle droids in your way, and jack the crab droid that crawls up the cliff side. Dash down the ramp and hop across the tall pillars toward the long demolished thruster on the other side of the chasm.

PSP NOTES

In the PSP version, a few jetpack-toting battle droids are present, while the crab droid is not.

ARTIFACT

An artifact is sitting atop one of the pillars as you cross the chasm. Grab it as you hop across!

Jump down on the other side of the chasm. As you land, four battle droids attack. Force Kill or Lightsaber Throw them in these tight quarters. Once you've reduced them to a pile of parts, a sabotage droid appears overhead. Double-jump onto it and jack it! Aim it at the weakened fence along the rear wall and launch it into the fence. The explosion creates a passage into the next area.

PSP NOTES

In the PSP version, only two battle droids are present.

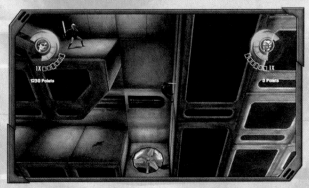

In the next corridor, destroy the chameleon droid in your way, then lightsaber-slide down the far wall. Leap backward into the next corridor before you reach the fan at the bottom. Take out one more chameleon droid, then slide down the next wall on the left.

PSP NOTES

In the PSP version, no chameleon droids are present.

As you slide down, leap backward again into another corridor. Walk right to one more tall shaft and slide down the right wall. Leap backward onto the wall behind you as you slide, and leap one last time into a new corridor on the right. Jack the chameleon droid at the corridor's end, and drop a few mines near the grating.

PSP NOTES

In the PSP version, no chameleon droids are present.

Pass through the opening in the corridor and rendezvous with Cad Bane and your kidnapped soldiers! When you arrive, all three men are engaged in a heavy firefight.

This clanker is no different than the first one you faced at the beginning of your journey. Trap its leg with the Force as it stomps at you, then climb up the leg to slash off its turret. Do this two times, and use its third turret to launch yourself on top of it and turn it into a useless pile of junk.

Rush down the ramp on the left, snagging the power-up as you go. Jack one of the super battle droids and fire on the others. Walk your clanker into their midst and use a jump attack to crush them all. After you destroy the enemies, two new waves of battle droids march in. Let Ahsoka handle one of the small groups while you destroy the other.

When the fight is over, Cad Bane leaps at the opportunity to fire at Anakin! The Jedi quickly deflects the fire back at the traitorous smuggler and knocks him to the floor. After disarming the scum, the group comes under heavy fire from the Separatists again.

Pounce on the sabotage droids that appear, and use them against the other droids as they march into battle. After destroying all the droids in the center of the bay, a huge octuptarra stomps into the center of the bay!

Rather than stick around and get blasted to pieces, Bane offers his ship as an escape vehicle. Rather than escape with just his hide, Bane insists on taking his bounty too. And though Skywalker doesn't know what's in the box, he knows it's important enough to keep with him rather than leave for the Separatists. Still, it's a long way to Cad Bane's ship, and someone has to carry the large box. It might as well be Bane.

ARTIFACT

An artifact is sitting on the top of the overhang on the left. Pick it up after destroying the super battle droids.

PSP AND WII NOTES

In the PSP and Wii versions, the artifact is below the overhang, not on top of it.

Cover Fire: Ryloth—Mission 11

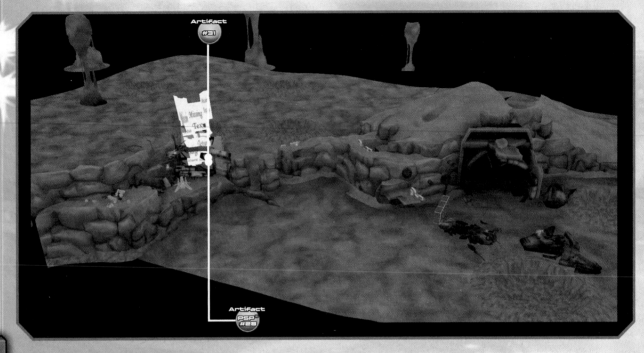

Artifact #31

Artifact PSP #28

From up on that ridge we'll be able to cover the whole area

As Anakin Skywalker, Ahsoka Tano, and Cad Bane set out to Bane's ship, the Jedi General ordered the two rescued clones to gain an elevated position where they can cover the escaping trio.

NOTE

During this mission, you take control of a clone trooper.

A Better Shot Higher Ground Provides

Dash right to a short wall and immediately take cover behind it. Open fire on the chameleon droids on the other side of the wall and take them out. Rush out from your cover and grab the explosive grenades on the left, then hurl them down at the enemies in the canyon below.

Before hopping down to the lower canyon, restock on explosive grenades. Drop down into the canyon and take the fight to the droids on the far right side of the area. When the crab droid climbs up the side of the cliff, greet it with a few grenades, then explore the crashed ship at the far right.

PSP NOTES

In the PSP version, there is no crab droid present here.

96

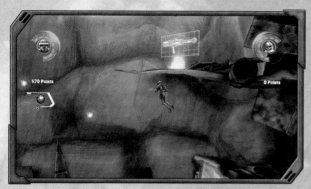

Use your jetpack to boost up the crashed ship, grabbing point spheres as you go. Follow the wreckage left, up the cliff side, to a small platform.

PSP NOTES

In the PSP version, no point spheres are located here.

ARTIFACT

As soon as you jetpack onto the crashed ship, grab the artifact from atop the wreckage!

Grab the rocket launcher on the small ledge and blow up the large wall on the right. Dash right, past the fallen wall, and greet several battle droids with blaster fire as they zoom in on various pillars ahead of you. Clear out the battle droids in your way, and turn left to locate the octuptarra on the distant left.

PSP AND WII NOTES

In the Wii and PSP versions, there is no rocket launcher or wall in this location.

Blast it to bits with several rockets as you carefully trek right across the pillars. Continue moving right, grabbing more rocket launchers and power-ups as you go. You may find it safer to fire with your hand blasters while strafing.

Stop when you reach a small hill on your far left, and open fire on the battle droids as they storm over the hill. When the droideka rolls over the hills, target them first and wipe them out quickly.

Hurl rockets at the approaching super battle droids and obliterate them before they can get all the way down the hill.

NOTE

A Droid Demolition challenge appears after destroying all of the droids that storm down the hill.

Continue moving right, past the hill, to a canyon surrounding a large circular tunnel. Switch to your blasters and immediately turn left toward the octuptarra that saunters out of the tunnel. If sabotage droids appear overhead, blast them while strafing, then turn back on the octuptarra. Continue firing on it until you bring it down.

With the area clear, you're finally in a higher position to cover the generals' escape!

Anybody Out There? Juma-9-Mission 9

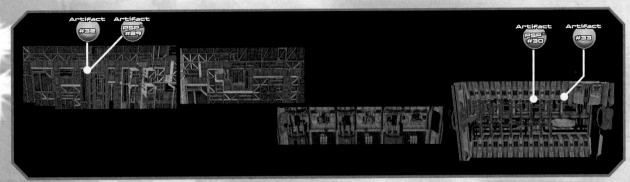

Back on the Juma-9 space station, Masters Fisto and Windu search for their missing comrades, Anakin Skywalker and Ahsoka Tano. Together, with the help of Switch, the heroic clone trooper, they search the station for their missing friends.

NOTE

Unleash your lightsaber as Kit Fisto during this mission!

Work as One, the Two of You Must

In the corridor, approach the malfunctioning platform on the right. Wait for Master Windu to lock the platform in place with the Force, then jump into the shaft beneath the now-removed platform. Lightsaber-slide down the shaft and grab the point spheres as you go.

Walk right and stab the console in the corridor with your lightsaber. The console deactivates the electrical field in the corridor above you. Wall-bound up the next shaft to the top level, and rejoin Master Windu. Make a right at the corridor and swing across the three poles to the other side.

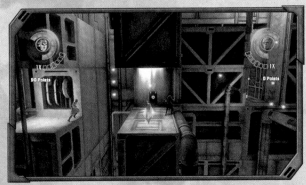

Jump over the next tall shaft, and turn right at the next platform. Leap over to the next area and jump down the shaft at the far end. At the base is a door blocked by an electrical field. Turn left and swing from the nearby pole onto a small platform with another computer console.

NOTE

There is a Droid Demolition challenge on the top level, just before you reach the electrified door below.

Bust the point crystal near the console, then sabotage the console to deactivate the electrical field blocking the doorway

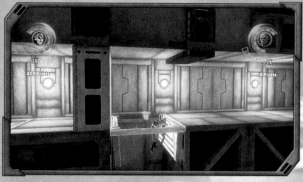

at the base of the shaft. Return to the door and go through into the next area.

ARTIFACT

To collect an artifact, jump left from the platform with the console, then follow a long winding pipe into a tall shaft. Jump from the pipe onto a small ledge on the left, then swing across three poles toward a dead-end wall. Lightsaber-slide down the wall to grab the artifact, then jump onto the pole to swing back to safety.

Bounce up the tall shaft at the end of the next corridor, then lightsaber-slide down to the lower level. As you slide down,

jump backward into a small niche containing a point crystal. Break it, then jump into the lower-level passage.

Slice the computer console in the corridor to deactivate the electrical field blocking the shaft ahead. Your companion holds up the wall for you to cross underneath. Do the same for your companion. Dash right until you reach a hatch, and use the Force to lift it out of the way. Watch for chameleon droids that can interrupt you if you're not careful.

Step onto the platform on the other side and the hatch closes behind you. Turn around to lift it with the Force and allow Master Windu to join you. When you attempt to open the next door, the platform gives way and sends you both plummeting into the next sector.

You both land on a large floating asteroid that slowly moves through the asteroid-demolition sector. Stay near its center as it floats into a large circular area surrounded by cutting laser beams. The beam emitters rise out of the area below, creating a series of pillars with point spheres on them. Either jump from pillar to pillar, staying ahead of the beams as they fire and collecting the point spheres, or stay put on the asteroid to avoid danger. Once all the cutting beams have finished firing, the asteroid begins to move again.

This time it stops in front of a large red force field. Jack one of the sabotage droids nearby and launch it into the shield generator on the far left wall. When the red field drops, the asteroid begins to move along again. Repeat this process across two more series of cutting beams and another red field until you reach the next section.

99

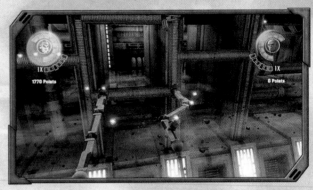

CAUTION

If you do grab the point spheres from the cutting beams, stay ahead of the beams before they fire. The usually fire twice, one by one, then finish by firing all at once. You can usually round all of the beams twice before needing to jump back onto the asteroid to dodge the beams when they fire simultaneously.

PSP AND WII NOTES

In the Wii and PSP versions, you don't need to move off the asteroid until you reach the next room.

This arm rises to meet one on the right, while another arm shifts left and right above it. Jump right onto the next arm, and stay on it as it shifts right, down, and right again. Walk out to the tip of the arm and wait for it to meet with the next arm on the right. When the next arm bends left toward you, leap onto it.

The next sector is the mineral-extraction area. It contains dozens of cutting beams that shift up, down, left, and right, across a long rectangular room. Jump onto the nearest beam and ride it as it moves down and to the right. Stay near the base of the moving arm (where it attaches to the wall), and jump from it to the next long arm below and to the right.

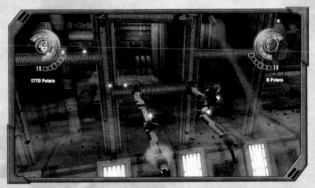

Ride the arm up, then jump onto the next arm on the right. Jump right, onto the next arm, then one more time to the arm that stays in place but bends left and right.

PSP AND WII NOTES

In the Wii and PSP versions, this room is a platform with points that connect to a floating lift that you need to get onto. An artifact is located atop some crates right before the floating platform. There is no mission challenge present.

Walk out to the firing end of the long arm and wait for it to bend to the right just as another arm on the right bends to the left. Jump right onto the next arm, then ride the arm as it bends right again toward another firing beam that bends left. As this arm shifts right along the wall, it also bends to the right. Double-jump onto the next arm, which stays straight but slides up and down along the wall.

Creep out to the firing end of the arm, and wait for it to bend right. As it does, it also bends up a little. Jump onto the next arm and ride it all the way up.

ARTIFACT

An artifact is located near the firing end of this arm. Walk out to grab it as the arm straightens and rises along the wall.

Finally, leap onto the final arm on the left!

NOTE

There is a Point Panic challenge at the base of the final firing beam.

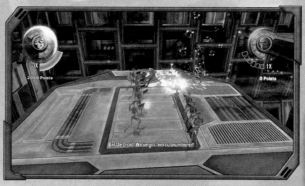

The arm on the left stays in place, so wait for the arm you're on to straighten, then double-jump left onto the next stationary arm. Leap left again onto the next arm and ride it down and to the left. Walk out to the arm's firing end and wait for it to bend left. Double-jump onto the next arm on the left and quickly scamper to the arm's base near the wall.

Wait for a large floating platform to rise to the arm you're on, then double-jump onto it. Stay near the center of the platform as it floats down and to the right. Grab the yellow power-up as it floats by, and crush the magna guard that attacks from the left. When the troop of battle droids zooms in, run your lightsaber through them and use jump attacks to crush them all at once. Alternatively, you can droid-jack the magna guard and use it to defeat the battle droids.

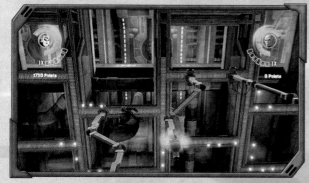

Ride it up and to the left, then leap onto the next arm. Walk out to the firing end and wait for it to bend left and down a bit. When it does, leap down onto the arm on the left below, and ride the tip of the arm up and to the left.

PSP AND WII NOTES

In the Wii and PSP version, the only enemies you'll encounter is a swarm of chameleon droids that attack midflight. Luckily you don't have to kill any of them; you just have to wait them out.

Continue riding the platform across the long room and stay near its center. When the sabotage droids surround the platform, jack one of them and launch it at the others. If you miss, use Force Blasts to knock them out of the air.

When you reach the next stop, break the point crystal on the left, and Force Blast the magna guards off the tiny platform. If they resist your Force Blast, jack them and send them flying off.

When the platform begins moving again, get near the far edge, facing the wall of cutting beams, and wait for another platform to float by. When the battle droids on the opposite platform begin to fire rockets at you, bounce them back with the Force and blow them up. When you finally reach the end of your travels on the platform, Switch manages to locate the two missing Jedi; they're sealed in a loading bay of the station!

With the missing Jedi found, all that is left is to find out what the Separatists were after in the station. Unfortunately, Switch can't find that information from his current location and instead needs to access the Communication Room terminals.

Rescue Mission: Juma-9-Mission 10

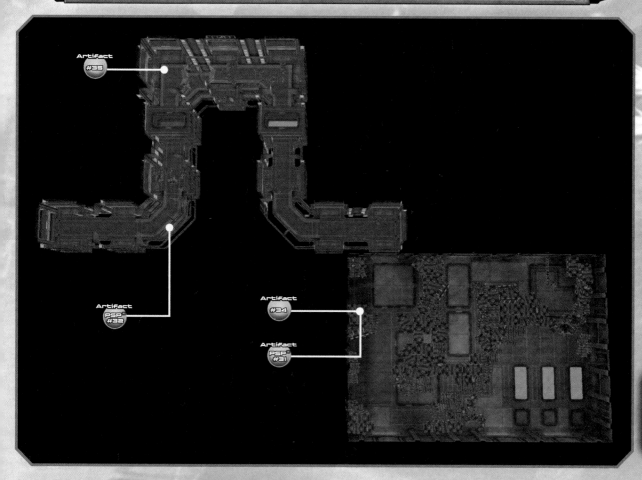

Artifact #33

Artifact PSP #32

Artifact #34

Artifact PSP #31

When Private Switch locates the missing Jedi, he relays the information to two clones on the other side of the station. The two troopers are the closest to Obi-Wan and Plo's location.

NOTE

During this mission, you assume control of a clone trooper. You will patrol the station on an AT-RT.

Even Jedi Need Rescuing at Times

Slowly march forward, toward the large hatch along the far wall. As you approach, a small squad of battle droids storms out from the hatch. Blast them to pieces, then aim at the crab droids that crawl down the far wall.

PSP NOTES

In the PSP version, spider droids replace the crab droids in this area.

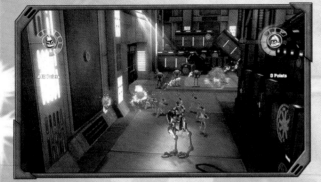

Turn left behind the boxes near the group of battle droids to find the next artifact! Jump over the lower boxes up to the ledge and you'll see the artifact there.

Take them out, then blast the spider droid perched on the top left. Make a sharp right as you near the hatch and obliterate the battle droids and super battle droids in the next section of the cargo bay. Hug the right wall as you approach to avoid the incoming fire from the droids around the right corner.

After clearing a path, enter the large, wide-open bay and turn right. Several more droids hide behind crates for cover. Burn them down and hop over the crates as several droideka rise up from the lifts below the bay. Hit them with several rounds from your blaster cannon and wipe them out! After destroying the droideka, a group of battle droids comes out of the blast doors.

NOTE

Once you've dealt with the battle droids, a Droid Demolition challenge appears at the center of this section.

Make a right, past the fallen droideka, and hop over the small wall of crates in your way. As you cross the wall, fire on the next few droideka ahead and dispatch them before they can do any damage.

Turn right at the corner and demolish the next few battle droids that approach from afar. Enter the passage behind the demolished droids and make a left.

March down the long corridor, destroying battle droids as you go until you reach a wall made of burning crates. Step on the platform in front of the wall and ride it up to the next level. Crush the gold droideka in your way and turn left at the next corner.

Open fire on the battle droids that march in from the right, then hop down the hole onto the area below. Turn left after landing and waste the droideka on the left.

ARTIFACT

An artifact is located inside the hangar on the right immediately after landing. Bust the crates inside and grab it!

PSP NOTES

In the PSP version, two spider droids replace the droideka, and the artifact is at the last turn against the left wall.

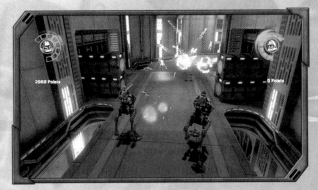

Follow the walkway left, past several more battle droids, and dispatch the super battle droids near the walkway's next turn.

PSP NOTES

In the PSP version, there are also some destroyer droids right before the final doorway.

When you reach the end of the corridor, you find Masters Kenobi and Koon trapped behind a large red force field. When you inform them that Mace Windu and Kit Fisto are heading for the communications room, the two Jedi promise to rendezvous with you there.

Vital Escort: Juma-9-Mission 11

Artifact
#36

Artifact
PSP
#21

PSP NOTES

You won't play this level in the PSP version. Please skip to Bad Company: Ryloth—Mission 12.

As Mace Windu and Kit Fisto journey across the space station, they encounter more Separatist resistance. If they're going to get any more information form the space station, they must escort Switch to the communications room safely!

NOTE

During this mission, you control Mace Windu.

Droid Parts, This Space Station Needs

Rush out of the lane of crates to a large, wide-open cargo bay. When the crab droids come crawling out, jack one of them and use its shock-wave attack to crush the battle droids in the bay.

ARTIFACT

There is another artifact located high above the cargo bay, atop a wall of crates. Jump off a crab droid to reach it!

Turn right after destroying all the droids in the first section of the bay, and quickly jump up the crates in the top left corner. Grab the red power-up, then take the fight to the droids in the lower hangar bay. Use the crab droid to demolish the smaller, weaker battle droids.

After taking out the first batch of droids, a vulture droid stops by for some fun. Allow Fisto to lock both of its legs down with the Force (or do it yourself), then climb atop the droid and stab its head with your lightsaber!

NOTE

After taking out the vulture droid, a Takeover Takedown challenge appears near the center of the bay.

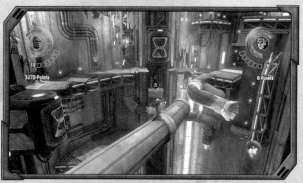

The explosion from the vulture droid blasts a hole in the far wall. Go through the hole into the next section, then ride the elevator down to the lower level.Climb the fallen pipe and follow it right, to a broken section of the pipe. Use the Force to bend the other side of the pipe into place, and cross to the other side.

ARTIFACT

An artifact is located underneath the platform after you cross the long pipe. Lightsaber-slide down the wall on the right and grab it, then wall-bound back to the platform above.

Slip into the niche on the platform across the pipe, and wall-bound to the top level. Swing left onto the top of the elevator, and hop down onto its other side. Follow the walkway to another elevator, and ride it up to the higher level.

Take the walkway on the left to another niche in the wall, and bounce up to the next level. Use the Force to remove the debris blocking your path on the left, then jump on the elevator below to ride it all the way up.

The first few waves of enemies are regular battle droids. Destroy the droids with lightsaber combos and Force Blasts. When the super battle droids come marching in, jack one and use it to blast the others.

Either take the pipe on the left or sneak onto the ledge on the right. Both paths lead to an elevator on the far right.

Fend off the next few waves long enough for a crab droid to come in. When it does, Force Kill it and the other droids. Hold out long enough for Switch to finish on the first console and move on to the second console on the room's right.

The first wave of droids that marches out on this side are super battle droids. Jack one and blast the others. When Switch is done, he'll move to the third computer console, near the center of the room.

Switch sabotages the console on the right, at which point you can ride the nearby elevator up. When you reach another elevator nearby, hit the elevators with a Force Blast and destroy them. Hop on the other elevator and take it higher. Continue hopping elevators until you reach the entryway to the next corridor.

Go through and enter the communications room. When you do, Switch immediately starts hacking into the computer on the left. Cover him while he works, and destroy the droids that approach from the left and right.

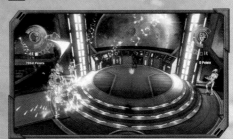

While he works on the center console, use Force Blasts and jump attacks to demolish the attacking droids. After you fend off several waves of enemies, Switch manages to hack the third console.

NOTE

A Droid Demolition challenge appears near the center console after you fight off all the droids.

Switch uncovers a curious scan record. Whoever used the scanners last didn't look for minerals in the surrounding asteroids; instead they searched for a particular energy frequency found on Ryloth. Before your group can get more information, Switch manages to turn the lights

back on in the comm room. When the Jedi turn around, they find that they're surrounded by numerous droids!

Returning the Favor: Juma-9-Mission 12

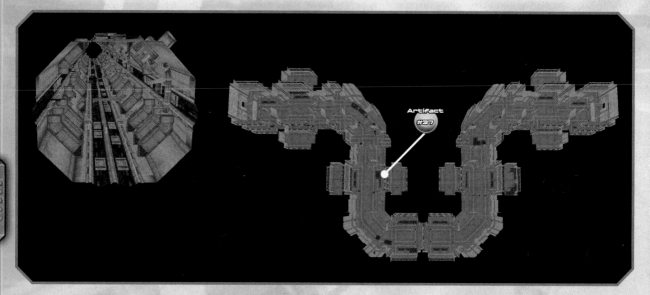

Artifact #37

Elsewhere on the space station, Masters Kenobi and Koon speed down the station halls empty-handed.

Since they lost their lightsabers in battle earlier, they've nothing to rely on but the Force....

 NOTE

Back in control of Master Kenobi, be prepared to fend off Separatist droids with nothing but the Force!

A Powerful Weapon the Force Can Be

Approach the gap in the walkway ahead and wait for the droids on the other side to begin firing rockets at you. When they do, bounce them back with the Force and blow them up! When the other side of the gap is clear, run across the small ledge against the left wall to the gap's other side.

Force Blast the next group of droids farther down the walkway and make a left. At the next gap, dash across the left ledge again, and use a Force Blast to hurl the super battle droids into the mines on the ground nearby.

Grab the power-up inside the large room on the left, then rush back out and hurl a powerful Force Blast at the approaching battle droids.

NOTE

After destroying all the droids in this area, a Droid Demolition challenge pops up.

Make a left after taking out all the enemy forces, and follow the walkway to another large group of battle droids. This time, use the Force to hurl the mines toward them and make short work of clankers.

Go to the walkway's end, where you'll find a dead end. When the chameleon droids start to appear and disappear, move to the center of the dead end, and hurl the mines they drop at them before they disappear again. Once you've destroyed all the chameleon droids in the dead end, the far hatch opens.

Dash into the next corridor, and follow it until a group of super battle droids marches out of a hatch on the left. Back away and grab the power-up on the walkway's right side. Wait for the chameleon droids to appear, then use Force Blasts to blow up all the droids.

ARTIFACT

As soon as the droids are destroyed and the camera turns, move to the boxes on the right, on the opposite wall of the door that opened. Behind these boxes is an artifact!

Take out the squad of battle droids that marches in from behind you, then cross the next gap on the right. Pick up the power-up on the right, and use the Force to blow up the rocket-launching battle droids across the next gap. Then cross to the other side.

Make a left into the small hangar, and hop on one of the STAP vehicles. Ride it out into the next section of the station.

In the next section, you must fly the STAP up a long, straight elevator shaft lined with point spheres. Stay near the center of the shaft to dodge the falling elevators that come barreling toward you. If you need to dodge two falling elevators at once, veer to the far left or right of the shaft until you're almost parallel to the side walls. Alternatively, you can just stick to one side of the elevators the whole way. You'll get fewer points, but you'll be safe the entire time.

When you reach the shaft's end, you'll turn into a small elevator exit to find Mace Windu and Kit Fisto engaged in battle!

As Obi-Wan Kenobi and Plo Koon arrive, they find that Mace Windu and Kit Fisto are surrounded on all sides. Rather than join the fight without a lightsaber, Kenobi breaks the window, blowing the droids out into space.

Bad Company: Ryloth-Mission 12

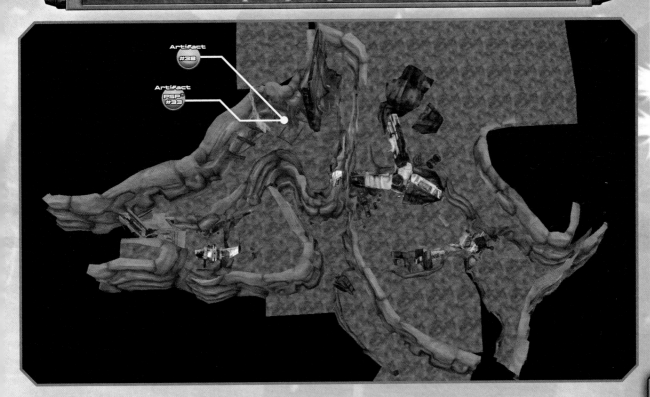

Artifact #38

Artifact PSP #33

Back on Ryloth, Jedi Knights Anakin Skywalker and Ahsoka Tano escort Cad Bane across the demolished landscape as Bane carries his precious cargo to his ship. Of course, nothing can go smoothly, as they are attacked by Separatist forces with each step they take!

NOTE

During this mission, you play as Anakin Skywalker.

Trust Cad Bane You Should Not

Rush the three super battle droids on the right while Bane cowers behind a small rock with his precious cargo. Jack one of the droids, and blast the other two to bits. After destroying the first three, turn left and hit the next wave of droids with a Force Blast as they approach.

PSP NOTES

In the PSP version, only one super battle droid will be present here.

NOTE

A Droid Demolition challenge appears as soon as you finish off the droids.

While you demolish the next few waves of droids, Bane leaves his cover and carries the box across the battlefield to the right. Wait for the spider droids to crawl up the cliff side, and crush them with jump attacks.

PSP AND WII NOTES

In the Wii and PSP versions, there is no mission challenge here.

 Jack one of the spider droids, and blast the nearby pile of debris blocking your path.

Double-jump over the broken wing blocking your path, then turn around and Force Push it down to bridge the gap. This allows Bane to carry his cargo across the gap.

ARTIFACT

There is an artifact located on the small perch along the right wall. To grab it, wall-bounce up the tall shaft, lightsaber-slide down the wall on the left, and leap backward onto the ledge to grab it.

 Rush into the next area, past the now-open hole in the wall, and rush the next group of droids. Take out the super battle droids first, then wipe out the battle droids and chameleon droids as they appear.

While you battle the droids below, your clone soldiers clear a path from above. Jump up the sloping incline against the far cliff and climb all the way up.

Run left along the wall and follow the small beam out over the group of droids below. Grab the red power-up at the end of the beam, and drop down on the droids below. Slash them to bits, then use Force Blasts against the sabotage droids that appear. With the sabotage droids gone, use the Force to disable the droideka shields and crush them with lightsaber combos.

Turn right and bounce the rockets back at the battle droids across the gap. When the crab droids rise from the edge of the cliff, crush them with jump attacks before they can cause any damage.

After destroying all the crab droids, the cowardly Bane comes stumbling down the ramp on the left. Use the Force to move a large piece of crashed ship into place and bridge the gap across the small chasm ahead. Cross the chasm and go down the cliff side to Bane's ship.

113

Scrapyard Scrap: Ryloth—Mission 13

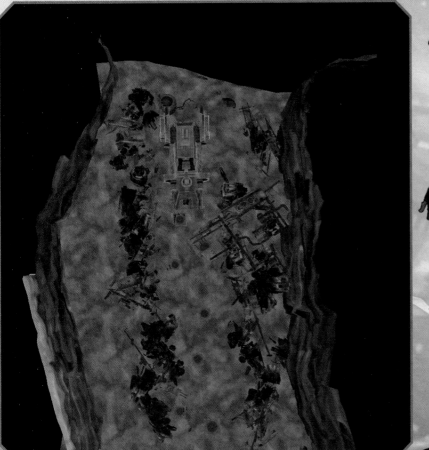

PSP NOTES

You won't play this level in the PSP version. Please skip to Act 3.

Upon reaching Bane's ship, Anakin senses something close by. Whatever it is, it's not good. He inspects the nearby wreckage, turning his back on the traitorous Bane just long enough for the smuggler to draw his gun.

Before Bane can blast Skywalker in the back, an old friend bursts out of the wreckage! It's Kul Teska, and he's after Bane's cargo. As Teska bursts out, a piece of debris knocks Bane's weapon out of his hand. He may not have gotten shot in the back, but now he's got to worry about the Skakoan!

Bothersome, Kul Teska Is

When the battle begins, keep an eye on Teska as he floats overhead. When he rushes at you like a cannonball, dash out of the way or block him with your lightsaber. Continue dodging Teska's cannonball attack until he tries to blow you up with rockets or get you with his grappling hand.

Hold your position and bounce his rockets back at him with the Force. After a few rocket blasts, Teska comes crashing down to the middle of the area. Rush the fallen Skakoan and let your lightsaber fly! Cut into him with combos and chop off as much of his health as you can. Repeat this process until you've depleted the yellow section of his Health bar.

After you chop down Teska's health, he traps you in a spherical force field!

NOTE

Once Anakin and Ahsoka are trapped, you gain control of two clone troopers to continue the fight.

The Jedi and clones give chase, but Teska takes off before they can reach him. To make matters worse, Bane escaped during all of the commotion!

Run around the battlefield and dodge Teska's grapple attacks. As soon as he launches his grappling arm at the ground, roll away from it. If you don't, he'll slam into the ground and crush you. While he's in the air, shoot him with your blasters.

Dash around the area, blasting him as he zooms about. When he stops, continue to blast him. Keep peppering him with blaster rifle fire until he loses all of the orange section of his Health bar.

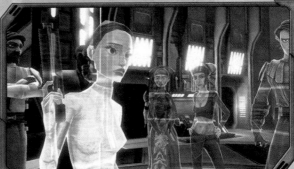

When he realizes he's bitten off more than he can chew, Teska retreats into Bane's ship and takes the cargo with him! Before leaving, he begins to shrink the force field around Anakin and Ahoska. The clone troopers quickly deactivate the force field, freeing the two Jedi.

Once all the dust settles, the Jedi link up through a communication relay. Plo Koon, Mace Windu, Kit Fisto, and Obi-Wan Kenobi are finally safe. Back on the Juma-9 space station, Switch found a message in the transmission buffers. It's from Kul Teska to Count Dooku—they plan on collapsing the Naboo sun!

Shortly thereafter, Senator Amidala sends a transmission that she's located a Separatist base on the Behpour near the Naboo sun. Your next move is clear—to Behpour.

ACT 3

A planet in peril! While investigating a threat to her homeworld of Naboo, Senator Amidala disappears after she discovers a Separatist base hidden within the system.

The Jedi Council determines it is part of the same plot they've been unraveling in the Outer Rim, a terrible new gravity weapon with enough firepower to collapse a star.

A planet in peril! When investigating a threat to her homeworld of Naboo, Senator Amidala disappears after she discovers a Separatist base hidden within the system. The Jedi Council determines it is part of the same plot they've been unraveling in the Outer Rim, a terrible new gravity weapon with enough firepower to collapse a star.

With time running out, Anakin Skywalker and Obi-Wan Kenobi head for the planet Behpour to lead an all-out assault on the facility and disable the doomsday weapon before it can be unleashed on an unsuspecting galaxy....

Distraction Action: Behpour–Mission 1

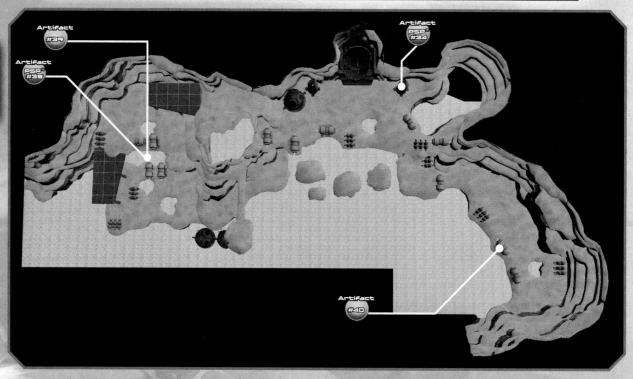

Artifact #39

Artifact PSP #34

Artifact PSP #35

Artifact #40

It's the only way I know how, General.

As all the Republic forces convene on the Behpour surface, they begin to review their plans for stopping the Separatist attack on the Naboo system. While Anakin Skywalker and Obi-Wan Kenobi prepare to disable the shields, Clone Trooper Rex and his men will create a diversion elsewhere on the planet.

NOTE

During this mission, you will take control of Commander Rex.

From the Real Assault, You Must Distract the Separatists

Slowly stomp your AT-RT left and blast the battle droids in your way. When the small hatches along the right wall slide open, aim at them and destroy the super battle droids that march out.

Your job, however, is not only to destroy the separatist droids, but also to create a distraction. So target the large tanks at the end, next to the doors, and blow them up.

Pop all of them, then stomp over to the large circular platforms over the acidic gasses below. Hop across the platforms to the other side, where several more droids are camped out.

ARTIFACT

There is an artifact hidden inside the tank next to the first breakable platform. Blast it a few times until it blows up, then grab the artifact before proceeding into the Behpour station.

On the other side of the acid river, several droids wait to ambush you. Hop down from your elevated position and immediately take out the crab droid on the left. Target the super battle droids next, then blast down the battle droids.

ARTIFACT

There is another artifact hidden inside the tank on the far right corner, just past the two hatches along the wall. Blow it open after taking out the droids, then grab it before you continue.

PSP AND WII NOTES

In the Wii and PSP versions, there are no crab droids on this level.

At the end of the area is a large circular platform supported by four beams. Blast the beams to bring the platform down, then hop up the rubble to the area above. Blast the battle droids on the area above, then take out the spider droid ahead of you.

PSP NOTES

In the PSP version, there is no spider droid at this location.

NOTE

There is a Droid Demolition challenge in the lower right corner of the area. Hop to it, after climbing up the first fallen platform.

After taking out the droids, target the large fuel cells on the right and blast them! Destroy all the tanks in the area; this creates a big enough distraction while...

After taking out the spider droid, blast the pillars supporting the platform on the right, and climb the rubble onto the next area. Stomp through the alley on the right, and enter the next area. Blow up the battle droids on the far right and take them out first.

PSP AND WII NOTES

In the PSP version, no spider droid is present. Also, In both the Wii and PSP versions, this level concludes when you defeat all the STAPs that come out of the structure.

Low Profile: Behpour-Mission 2

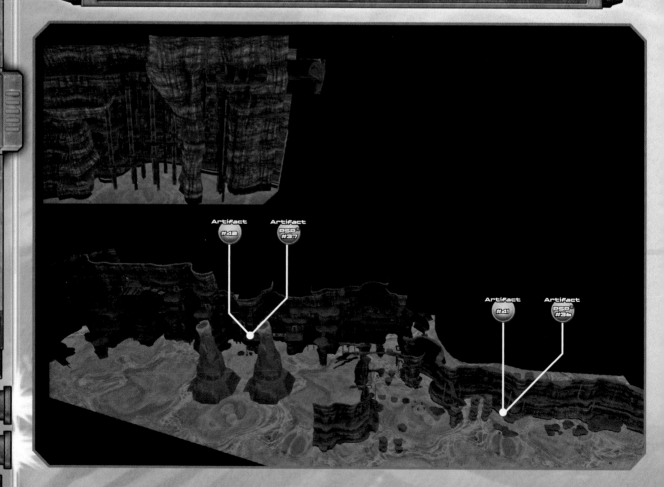

Artifact #42

Artifact PSP #37

Artifact #41

Artifact PSP #36

Meanwhile, elsewhere on the Behpour surface, Anakin Skywalker and Obi-Wan Kenobi prepare to infiltrate the Separatist base. As they approach the base, Skywalker's thoughts turn to something—or rather someone—else, rather than his mission.

On the Mission, a Jedi Must Focus Completely

Set out to infiltrate the Behpour base, and jump across the rock platforms over the acid river. When you reach the large gap between platforms, wait for the smaller platforms to rise up from the acid river and quickly jump across.

At the next large gap, the platforms float down the river, slowly passing you. Carefully but quickly, double-jump across the platforms as they float by until you reach the opposite end.

ARTIFACT

There is another artifact located on the far right wall of the cliffs. To reach it, first cross the floating platforms to the left, then hop back across them to the right, toward the distant wall.

Hop left, across the small pillars, to the far wall on the base's left side. When you reach the far wall, jump across the green platforms jutting out from the wall. Swing across one small pole in the process, then land atop a long land bridge.

Follow it right to a large platform with a series of pipes on the left.

NOTE

There is a Point Panic challenge on the platform after crossing the land bridge!

PSP NOTES

There is no mission challenge in the PSP version.

Jump left and grab the pipe overhead. Swing from it to the long, winding pipe below, then follow the pipe to another long pole overhead. Swing from it to more pipes, and hop from pipe to pipe until you reach the next series of rock platforms on the left.

Double-jump across the platforms on the left, and swing across the next three poles to another large ledge. Creep out to its edge, then swing onto the pole on the left. Hoist yourself onto it, then walk right toward the far wall.

Turn left and face the next few poles. Swing across them to the large ledge on the left, and immediately Force Blast the droids that attack. Wait for a spider droid to crawl out of the hatch on the right, then jack it. Fire across the long, electrified beam on the left and blow up the electrical generator.

PSP AND WII NOTES

In the Wii and PSP versions, spider droids will appear from above and below and will crawl onto the ledge.

Once the generator is destroyed, the electrical field over the beam goes away. Dash across the beam onto the next ledge.

ARTIFACT

An artifact is located where the electrical generator used to be. Grab it after crossing the beam to the next ledge.

NOTE

There's another Point Panic challenge on the platform after crossing the beam!

PSP NOTES

There's no mission challenge in the PSP version.

Approach the cliff side, then bounce off the left wall onto the beam behind you. Swing from it to the right wall, and bounce up and back to another beam above you. Pull yourself up, then jump onto the platform on the left.

From here, double-jump onto the ledge on the left and follow it to a smaller rock outcropping along the cliff. Double-jump from the outcropping to the ledge on the left, and immediately destroy the super battle droids that come out of the nearby hatch.

Jump onto the pole on the left and grab on to it. From here, jump to the next pole and pull yourself onto it.

In the Wii and PSP versions, you'll start out this section already in the pipe section.

Jump onto the opposite wall and bounce onto the pole above you. Swing from the pole to the next platform, and blast the battle droids with the Force.

Jump across the three platforms on the left to a large, half-circle hatch. Destroy the two computer consoles flanking the hatch. Once you've hacked both consoles, a small battalion of super battle droids and battle droids march out of the hatch. Leap over their heads and come down on them with a jump attack.

Follow the pipe left to another support and slide down again. Repeat this down the next few pipes and supports until you reach the end of the cavern. Once you're there, you order your men to advance!

Enter the hatch and jump onto the wall on the left. Lightsaber-slide down to the point just before the break in the wall; then jump onto the wall behind you, and lightsaber-slide down a bit farther.

Leap back onto the wall on the right one last time, before the wall on the left ends. Hop onto the ledge below. Creep out onto the pipe on the left, then jump onto the long support on the right. Slide down the support to another pipe and hop onto it.

121

First Line of Advance: Behpour-Mission 3

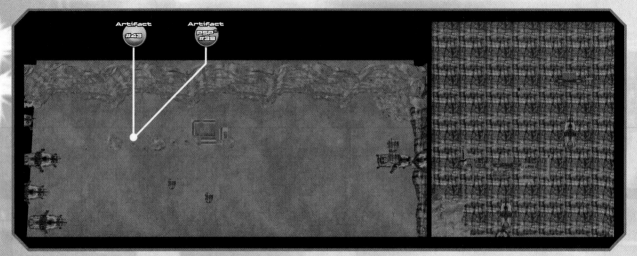

Artifact #43   Artifact PSP #38

Battles rage all over the Behpour surface. As soon as Anakin and Obi-Wan are in place, Mace Windu and Ahsoka Tano begin their advance on the base while riding an AT-TE.

NOTE

Congratulations, you get to fight alongside Mace Windu as Ahsoka Tano during this mission!

Only Once the Pieces Are in Place Should One Move

Ride the AT-TE toward the cliffs. When you reach the platforms on the left, double-jump onto them and crush the droids perched there.

ARTIFACT

There's another artifact on the second platform on the right. Grab it quickly before jumping back onto the AT-TE.

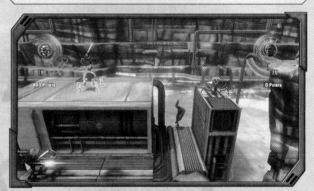

Hop back onto the AT-TE transport and ride it farther up the battlefield. Jump onto the next series of platforms on the left, and hop across them toward the spider droids perched atop the large structure on the right. Wall-jump up the side of the structure to its top, leaving Master Windu to handle the super battle droids. Crush the spider droid from above.

After destroying the first spider droid, hop onto the wall on the right, then double-jump onto the tall pillar. Destroy the gold spider droid atop the tall pillar, and wait for the AT-TE to pull up next to you.

NOTE

After taking out all the droids on the platform, a Droid Demolition challenge pops up near the computer console on the left.

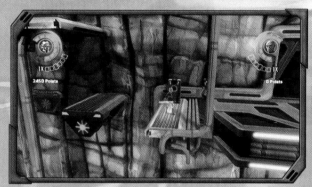

Ride your transport vehicle all the way up the cliff side, then wait for the battle droids to pull up on STAP vehicles. When they do, jack one of them and ride the STAP around the AT-TE as you clear out the rest of the droids. Alternatively, you can use Force Blast to eliminate them or to make them vacate the STAP vehicles.

Stab the console on the left with your lightsaber, and force the platforms on the left to begin popping out. Hop across the platforms as they pop out of the cliffs, then wall-bounce onto the platform above you.

When the AT-TE reaches the cliffs, it begins stomping up the cliff side. No sooner does it climb up the few hundred feet than it comes to a complete halt as a platform blocks its path. You automatically hop from your platform onto the one on the right. Bounce off the right wall toward the pole above and behind you, then swing onto the platform on the left.

Run your lightsaber through the super battle droids, and leave Master Windu to handle the smaller droids. Fend off the droideka as it rolls onto your platform, and force it off with a few good blasts.

Swing across the next few poles to the right, and wait on the final pole until the AT-TE climbs higher along the cliff side. When it reaches you, let go of your pole and land on the AT-TE. Ride the vehicle up the cliff wall until it reaches another series of platforms and poles on the right.

Grab the pole on the right and climb onto it. Wait for the bursts of fire between poles to stop, then leap across the poles to the next platform.

123

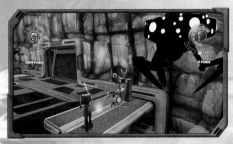

Let Mace Windu distract the droids on the platform while you destroy the console with your lightsaber.

Jump back onto the transport vehicle and ride it all the way up the cliff. At the cliff top is the base's shield. Now it's up to Anakin and Obi-Wan to bring down the shields....

After destroying the console, the platform retracts into the wall, clearing a path for the AT-TE.

Open Up: Behpour-Mission 4

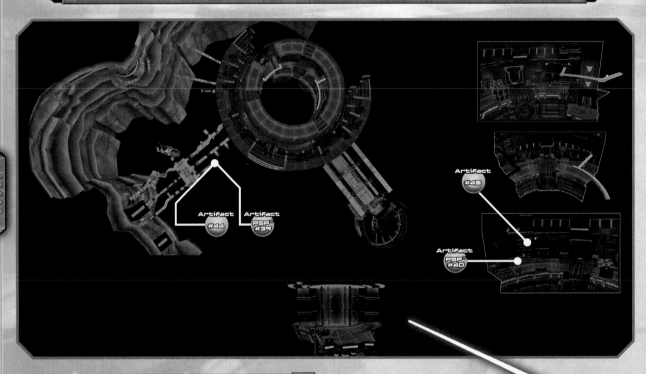

Artifact #44

Artifact PSP #39

Artifact #45

Artifact PSP #40

This isn't the time for one of your hunches.

As the battle rages on outside the base, Obi-Wan and Anakin prepare to destroy the base's shields from inside. Of course, as is usually the case, the duo approach their task with no real plan set in place....

As You Go Along, You Must Sometimes Make It Up

Turn right and approach the platform's edge. When the droids on the other side of the chasm begin firing rockets at you, bounce them back with the Force and blow them up. Hop along the maintenance droids floating in the chasm, then step onto the next platform.

Make a right and cross the long beam to a distant platform. Once there, use the two sabotage droids in the area against the large generators on the right.

PSP NOTES

The rocket-toting battle droids are not present in the PSP version. Also, super battle droids replace the sabotage droids.

NOTE

After taking down the generators, a Point Panic challenge pops up on the platform.

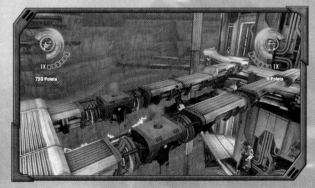

Cross the long beams on the right and reach the next platform.

ARTIFACT

An artifact is located on the broken beam all the way on the right. Grab it before you cross onto the next platform.

Grab the red power-up as you cross the beam, then turn left at the platform. Crush the battle droids in your way with a few lightsaber combos, then turn on the spider droids that crawl up the side. Use your lightsaber to hack the console on the left, and open the hatch leading inside the main base.

PSP NOTES

There is no red power-up present in the PSP version.

Turn right into the hatch and immediately take out the super battle droids. Turn right inside the long, circular room and fight your way past several battle droids. Grab the power-ups along the left wall as you go, and use the spider droids as weapons.

Continue moving down the right, demolishing droids as you go, until you reach a closed hatch with a checkpoint marker in front of it. Hold your ground near the center, and fend off the waves of droids as they attack. When you're done, proceed to the right again.

NOTE

After dispatching all the droid waves, a Takeover Takedown challenge appears near the center of the area.

ARTIFACT

An artifact is located high atop the ledge along the wall after passing the Takeover Takedown challenge.

PSP AND WII NOTES

In the PSP version, there is no mission challenge, and the artifact is located on the ground between two groups of exploding barrels, right before the room's exit. In the Wii version, the artifact is floating on a beam above the ground.

Stop at the next hatch and turn toward it. When it opens, crush the battle droids on the other side of the hatch. Jump-attack the spider droids before crossing the hatch and dashing up the long walkway.

About halfway up the walkway, a pair of magna guards attacks! Droid-jack one of them and turn its electro-staff on the other guard. Destroy the first two, then rush up the walkway and take out several more until you reach a platform with a tall force field.

PSP AND WII NOTES

In the Wii and PSP versions, when you reach the hatch, there are several battle droids, a spider droid, and two super battle droids inside a doorway outside the hatch. After you defeat them, slice the console to open the hatch. After you defeat four magna guards, the walkway collapses and pushes you into the final room.

PSP NOTES

In the PSP version, there will be no battle droids behind the hatch.

Destroy the first two magna guards that attack you, then rush to the right and Force Push the large wall switch into place. As soon as the first switch is in place, rush across the platform, leaving the new magna guards for Master Windu and Force Pushing the other switch into place. When it slides in, the force field in the center drops!

CAUTION

If you take too long popping in the second switch, the first one will pop back out of the wall!

Once the force field drops, push in the two wall switches on the interior into the wall, then drop the next small force field. When it's down, use a lightsaber attack to destroy the shield generator at the platform's center.

With the shield down, your next task is to locate and disable the gravity weapon! Of course, Senator Amidala is also somewhere in the station....

Zero Hour: Behpour-Mission 5

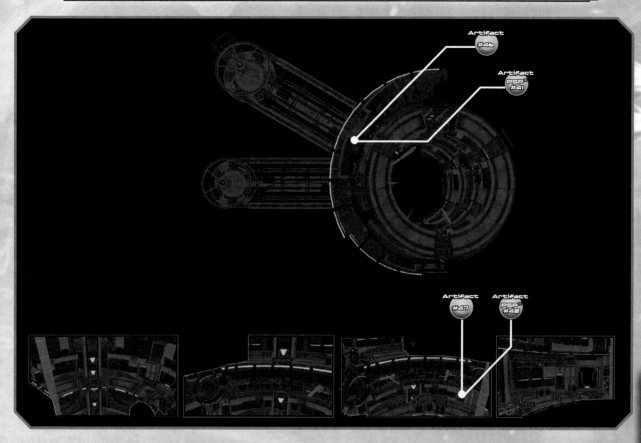

As the base's shield comes down, General Mace Windu sends his clones into the base! The troopers leap into the center of the base and immediately secure the entrance, allowing Mace and the young Padawan to leap into the fray.

NOTE

During this mission, you take control of Mace Windu, Jedi General extraordinaire!

From the Inside Out, You Can Destroy the Base

Approach the right edge of the platform and face the battle droids on the opposite platform. Wait for them to launch their rockets, then bounce them back with the Force. When the turbolift drops down from above, bridging the gap, rush onto it and jack one of the super battle droids. Use it to destroy the others.

Dash right across the station and battle your way to the electrified field. Hop over the right ledge onto one of the floating maintenance droids. Bounce right from droid to droid until you pass the electric field. Leap from the last droid onto a long beam, and wait for the large spinning wheel on the inside of the circular room to spin toward you. When it does, jump onto the bar attached to the wheel and quickly jump across the wheel to the next beam.

Continue jumping across floating droids, spinning wheels, and beams until you reach the other side of the large room. Hop onto a maintenance droid and ride it up, then jump forward, back onto the room's outer ring. Destroy the battle droids that rush in from the hatch along the outer wall.

PSP AND WII NOTES

In the Wii and PSP versions, after jumping on the maintenance droid, you'll need to maneuver through the pipes and gear. When you get back to the top, destroy the battle droids and spider droids so that a clone trooper will slice the console and open the door.

Rush out onto the walkway on the hatch's other side and sprint up the walkway, dispatching super battle droids as you go. When you reach the walkway's end,

perform a Force Blast to take out and disrupt the enemies across the way so they don't shoot you out of the air when you double-jump over the gap. After doing so, take the center of the platform.

ARTIFACT

There's an artifact located on the lower left level of the walkway, as soon as you pass through the hatch. Grab it before you continue.

Hold the center of the platform, and wait for the battle droids and super battle droids to attack, if you haven't defeated them yet. When they do, either knock them off the platform with Force Blasts or jack the more powerful droids to use against the smaller, weaker ones. After dispatching several waves of droids, take the long, winding platform on the left down to the ring section, which is high above another circular platform.

NOTE

A Droid Demolition challenge appears at the center of the platform as soon as you destroy all your droid attackers.

PSP NOTES

There is no mission challenge in the PSP version.

Jump down from the ring onto the area below.

Hop onto the STAP vehicle inside the large circular room, and zoom to the room's center as you blast the droids that rush out of the doors lining the outer wall. When the enemy STAPs rush out into the room's center, blast them out of your way and return to the droids on the outer rim. Fend off all the remaining droids until the room is yours.

NOTE

After taking out all of your enemies, a Droid Demolition challenge appears near the center of the room!

PSP NOTES

In the PSP version, you'll need to destroy only the super battle droids that come out of the doorway on the right side for the levels to complete. Also, there is no mission challenge.

129

Once again, hold your position near the platform's center, and Force Blast all the droids off the platform as they attempt to surround you. Turn left and follow the walkway up to the next section. When you reach the gap, swing across the pole above you to the other side.

Make a left at the walkway's end, and either run your lightsaber through the attacking droids, or Force Blast them off the walkway. After clearing the area of all enemies, slice the console on the left and open the hatch. Enter the next large room.

ARTIFACT

The next artifact is located right next to the entrance to this large room, behind a door that you must open from a control panel. When you enter this last room, move immediately to the right to see the panel (walk closer to the STAPs to bring the camera out more). After activating the panel, the door will open and you will see the artifact.

After you take the room, Anakin and Obi-Wan storm in, ready to join the battle. Rendezvous with them on the outer ring and plan your next step!

Exit Clearance: Behpour-Mission 6

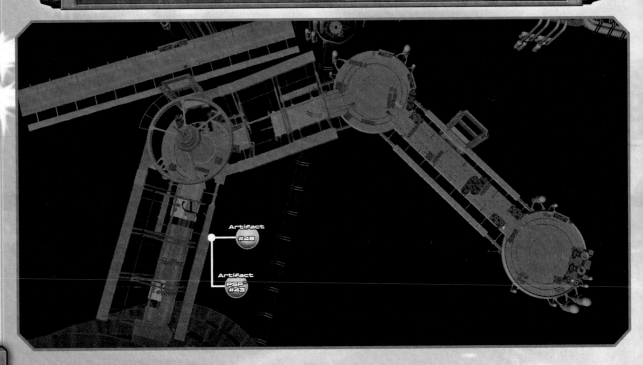

Artifact #43

Artifact PSP #43

As the plan almost comes to fruition, the clone troopers prepare to set up an evac zone. But as always, the Separatists make things much harder than they need to be.

NOTE

During this mission, you take control of a brave clone trooper.

Prepare for a Last Minute Escape, You Probably Should

As the mission begins, an explosion rocks the walkway ahead of you, nearly splitting it in two. Rush forward onto the walkway and boost-jump over the crates in your way with your blasters blazing.

ARTIFACT

There's an artifact on the walkway's lower right side, about halfway across. Grab it as you approach the end of the walkway.

Grab the minigun power-up on the walkway's lower left side, and boost over the gap ahead of you onto the large circular section at the walkway's end. Take cover behind the crates, and open fire on the attacking battle droids. Sweep the area left and right to get all of the battle droids, then grab the explosive grenades power-up from the platform's left side.

This time, stay behind the crates on the left and let the grenades fly at the super battle droids. After sweeping the area, make a right and approach the electrical fields blocking the right walkway. Allow your clone comrade to hack the console and lower the fields, then rush up the walkway toward a pair of droideka. Blow them up with grenades, then restock on the grenades from the station on the left.

Rush up the walkway, but before reaching the next platform, stop at the lip of the next area. Toss another grenade ahead of you at the group of droids on the other side.

Take out the first few super battle droids, then rush across the platform to the blaster power-up on the far right side. As soon as you pick it up, turn around and open fire on the crab droids behind you. Sweep left and right across the platform until you've destroyed every droid.

NOTE
Before leaving the first circular platform, a Droid Demolition challenge pops up!

PSP AND WII NOTES
In the Wii and PSP versions, you—not your companion—slice the console. Also, there's no mission challenge.

PSP NOTES
In the PSP version, there are two super battle droids on the walkway to the next area instead of destroyer droids. Also, there are rockets to the left on the lower walkway and grenades to the right.

NOTE
After taking out all the droids on this platform, a Droid Demolition challenge appears near the center of the area.

PSP AND WII NOTES
In the Wii and PSP versions, you'll need to hack another console to bring down an electrical field.

PSP NOTES
In the PSP version, there is no blaster power-up, no crab droids, and no mission challenge.

131

Make a right at the next walkway, and take cover behind the small wall of crates. Open fire on the crab droid ahead. If you still have explosive grenades, duck down onto the walkway's lower right section and hurl them over the edge onto the attacking droids.

When the vulture droid drops in on the platform's center, back away down the walkway and restock on rocket ammo. Blast the vulture droid with your rockets while strafing!

Speed across the walkway, blasting droids in your way until you reach a pair of electrical fields blocking your path. While your clone partner disables the fields, grab the rocket launcher on the right and aim it farther down the walkway. As soon as the fields come down, let a rocket fly at the droids ahead of you.

Speed to the walkway's end, and blast the battle droids lining the outer edge. Next, boost onto the large crates on the edge of the walkway to stay out of the magna guard's reach. Pop it with rockets from above to take it out.

Hit the vulture droid with three rockets. It soon falls, clearing the platform for an escape vessel. The clones have comes through as always!

A Skywalker Plan: Behpour-Mission 7

Anakin and Ahsoka have reached the station's main turbolift, but they aren't sure if they'll find the gravity weapon in time. As the duo descend deeper into the Behpour base, it becomes increasingly clear that even though Anakin doesn't have a plan, he does plan on finding and rescuing Senator Amidala.

NOTE

During this mission, you assume control of Anakin Skywalker.

By the Seat of His Pants, Young Anakin Likes to Fly

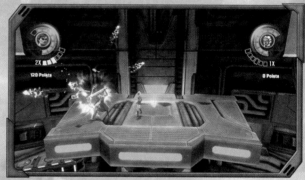

Stay near the center of the turbolift as it descends deeper into the base. When the battle droids drop in on you, take them out quickly with swift lightsaber strikes. At the first stop, dash right and destroy the droids with a few Force Blasts.

After demolishing the droids on the right, dash back across the lift and crush the clankers on the left. Sweep the area clean of all battle droids, then focus on the droideka.

PSP NOTES
There is no droideka on the left side in the PSP version, but there are a few battle droids.

Artifact
PSP
#44

Artifact
#49

Slice the console on the left and right of the lift to get it moving again, then hop back on and ride it farther down. This time, a small group of spider droids drops in on you from above. Use a series of jump attacks to take them all out.

PSP NOTES

In the PSP version, jetpack battle droids replace the spider droids.

Get the lift moving again, then ride it down to the next two levels. To avoid the cross fire from the droids on the left and right, stay near the lift's center as you descend. Stay swift on your feet to avoid getting blasted.

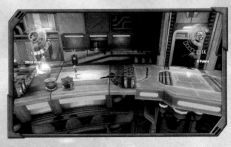

At the next stop, dash right and grab the yellow power-up near the far wall. Use a super battle droid to wipe out the other droids nearby, then sprint left and grab the power-up on the ledge along the far wall.

ARTIFACT

There's an artifact hidden behind the small crates in the top left corner of this level. Break the crates first, then grab the power-up before returning to the lift.

At the next stop, jump left and droid-jack the nearest crab droid. Use its shock-wave attack to take out the rest of the enemies nearby, then dash back across the lift to the right. Use quick lightsaber combos to crush the super battle droids in your way, then hack both consoles just as you did before. Once the turbolift gets moving again, hop on and go for a ride.

On the way down, a small group of battle droids flies onto your lift. Hit them with the Force and crush them quickly before reaching the next stop. Grab the red power-up on the left, and destroy all the droids there. Use jump attacks to disable the droidekas' shields, then jack them and use them against the other droids.

PSP NOTES

In the PSP version, spider droids replace the crab droids. Also, there isn't a red power-up or a destroyer droid.

NOTE

A Droid Demolition challenge appears on the right and left sides of the level, after you destroy all the droids on this level.

PSP AND WII NOTES

In the Wii and PSP versions, there is no mission challenge, and the artifact is located in front of the doorway in the middle of the lift at the third stop.

Cut through the battle droids on the far left, then hack the two consoles to get the lift moving again. Ride it down. As you do, a group of magna guards drops in from above. Jack them and attack the other guards with your magna puppet's electro-staff. Use jump attacks to finish off the guards on the walkway until you reach the final level.

Old Friends: Behpour-Mission 8

As Anakin and Ahsoka make their way to the Skakoan's gravity weapon, Count Dooku attacks the clones at the evacuation zone! He quickly destroys the evac transport ship, but not before Mace Windu and Obi-Wan Kenobi confront the traitorous Sith.

NOTE

During this mission, you take on Dooku and his magna guards as Mace Windu.

To Downfall Overconfidence Can Lead

As the battle against Dooku begins, the Sith Lord leaps away and takes refuge atop one of the large generators around the side of the platform. Leave Dooku for now and use a series of jump attacks to take out his magna guards. If you can't attack all of them at once, jack one of them and turn it on the others. Allow Master Kenobi to distract the guards while you attack them.

Once you've taken out all of Dooku's magna lackeys, he comes down from his perch and strikes. Attack him with lightsaber combos until he uses his Sith lightning. When he does, allow yourself to get zapped; Yoda then instructs you to redirect the lightning at one of the generators on the outside of the platform by swinging your lightsaber toward them.

As Dooku continues to fight, the generator charges the electricity and eventually overloads, sending a massive electrical blast out from the platform's center! When it does, the blast hits Count Dooku, dealing massive damage. Repeat this three times until Dooku's Health bar turns red.

Continue to redirect Dooku's lightning to the generators, and zap him with his own electrical charge. This time, however, you'll need to lure Dooku to the platform's center while the generators charge. After hitting him three more times, Dooku and the platform take enough damage to send them plummeting into the acid river below....

Old Enemies: Behpour—Mission 9

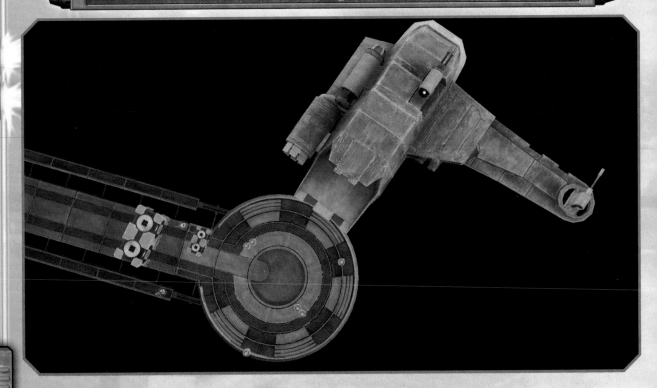

136

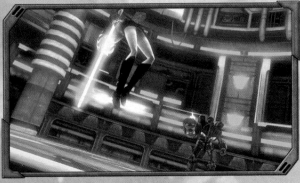

After reaching the bottom of the base, Anakin Skywalker and Ahsoka Tano finally come face-to-face with the Skakoan! He holds Senator Amidala hostage and threatens to use his gravity weapon to destroy the Naboo system. Before he can act on his threats, however, Anakin frees the Senator, and his Padawan takes action!

NOTE

During this final encounter, you play as Anakin Skywalker.

Once and for All, Finish This

As soon as Kul Teska leaps into the air and begins flying about, take the center of the platform. When he fires his beam at you, leap out of the way or block. Continue to dodge or block his laser-beam attacks until he tries to ram you with his cannonball attack.

After a short while, he'll summon several crab droids to help him crush you. Jack one of the crab droids, and use its shock-wave attack to bring Teska crashing down on the platform.

When he's down, rush the fallen Skakoan and let him have it! Continue this process until his Health bar is depleted to orange. After you dwindle down his health, Kul Teska flies higher into the ring section of the station.

PSP NOTES

In the PSP version, Kul Teska does not fly up to the higher section of the station.

NOTE

While you fight Kul Teska, the gravity weapon's firing sequence begins to power up!

With Teska stranded on the inner ring, you jump on the outer ring, just out of his reach. As Teska launches rockets at you, rush out of their way, then droid-jack the nearby sabotage droids and launch them at Teska. After several hits with the sabotage droids, Teska takes too much damage and is knocked back into his weapon's firing beam!

PSP AND WII NOTES

In the Wii and PSP versions, Teska shoots a laser at you instead of rockets.

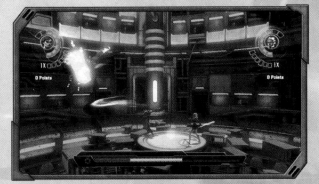

Step on the center of the ring, and ride the small circular platform up to the next level. As you do, a series of debris particles form around your small platform. Use the debris to dodge Teska's attacks or block with your lightsaber; then bounce his rockets back at him. Bring him crashing down on your platform again, then strike him with lightsaber combos.

After reducing Teska's health to red, he leaps back into the air, floating higher in the firing ring. Meanwhile, the firing sequence continues to charge! Before Teska can attack, someone steps in and blasts Teska's jet boosters, stranding him on the inner ring of the platform. It's Cad Bane, and he's finally gotten payback for Teska's earlier transgressions.

137

Seconds to Zero: Behpour—Mission 10

ARTIFACT

The final artifact is located about halfway through the tunnel (#50, PSP #45). Stay near the tube's center to avoid getting too far from it as you go.

While you were defeating Kul Teska, Senator Amidala was busy trying to disable his weapon. Though she came close to failing, she did disable it. As Anakin and Padawan Tano hop on STAP vehicles, Senator Amidala grabs a ride with Anakin. Whatever she did to the weapon is making the entire base self-destruct!

When you reach the end of the long tunnel, you emerge just in time to catch the escape vessel as it prepares to leave. As always, it's a last-minute escape after a successful mission....

Short and Fast

As soon as the mission begins, move toward the center of the firing tune, and follow the point spheres ahead. Carefully swerve left and right to avoid hitting the red firing beams, and dodge blaster fire coming from the combat that is still occurring in the structure.

Don't stray too far from the middle of the firing tube. As you near the end of the long tunnel, the beams will begin to rotate more quickly. Shift left and right, dodging the beams as you go until you reach the end.

UNLOCKABLES

Force Points are your key to all unlockables. Everything from mission ranks to unlockable cheats require you to accumulate and spend Force points. The following pages reveal everything you need to know about unlockables, Trophies, Achievements, and mission ranks!

TIP

The easiest way to unlock everything in a single play-through is to save up your Force points until you have about 30,000; then purchase the Combo cheat and keep it on. You'll profit nicely for doing so!

Mission Ranks

To attain a specific mission rank, you must accumulate the required Force points by mission's end. However, there are five missions that are the exception; they are time-based, so the quicker you finish, the better the rank:

My Name Is Kul Teska   Old Friends

It's a Trap   Old Enemies

Scrapyard Scrap

NOTE

The missions below are listed in the order you'll complete them.

Act	Name	Mission No.	Bronze	Silver	Gold	Platinum
Prologue	Master and Padawan	Ryloth 1	0+	1,000	2,000	3,000
Act 1	Powering up Resdin	Ryloth 2	0+	1,000	2,000	3,000
Act 1	Outpost Initiation	Ryloth 3	0+	1,000	2,000	3,000
Act 1	Rookie Rendezvous	Ryloth 4	0+	1,500	3,000	4,500
Act 1	Assault!	Juma-9 1	0+	2,000	4,000	6,000
Act 1	Power Reroute	Juma-9 2	0+	2,000	4,000	6,000
Act 1	Hazardous Infestation	Juma-9 3	0+	1,000	2,000	3,000
Act 1	Seek and Destroy	Ryloth 5	0+	2,000	4,000	6,000
Act 1	Emergency Evac	Ryloth 6	0+	2,500	5,000	7,500
Act 1	Out on Patrol	Ryloth 7	0+	1,500	3,000	4,500
Act 1	Missing in Action	Ryloth 8	0+	1,000	2,000	3,000
Act 1	S.O.S.	Juma-9 4	0+	1,000	2,000	3,000
Act 1	Abandon Ship!	Juma-9 5	0+	2,000	4,000	6,000
Act 1	My Name Is Kul Teska	Juma-9 6	270+ sec.	< 270 sec.	< 180 sec.	< 90 sec.
Act 2	Cliff Top	Azloc III 1	0+	500	1,000	1,500
Act 2	Ground Zero	Azloc III 2	0+	1,000	2,000	3,000
Act 2	Take It Back	Juma-9 7	0+	2,500	5,000	7,500
Act 2	Inside Out	Juma-9 8	0+	1,000	2,000	3,000
Act 2	Eye of the Storm	Azloc III 3	0+	1,000	2,000	3,000
Act 2	Guard Duty	Azloc III 4	0+	2,000	4,000	6,000
Act 2	It's a Trap	Azloc III 5	270+ seconds	< 270 sec.	< 180 sec.	< 90 sec.
Act 2	Enemies of My Enemies	Ryloth 9	0+	1,500	3,000	4,500
Act 2	Reunion under Fire	Ryloth 10	0+	1,000	2,000	3,000
Act 2	Cover Fire	Ryloth 11	0+	1,500	3,000	4,500
Act 2	Anybody Out There?	Juma-9 9	0+	1,500	3,000	4,500
Act 2	Rescue Mission	Juma-9 10	0+	2,500	5,000	7,500
Act 2	Vital Escort	Juma-9 11	0+	2,500	5,000	7,500

Act	Name	Mission No.	Bronze	Silver	Gold	Platinum
Act 2	Returning the Favor	Juma-9 12	0+	1,000	2,000	3,000
Act 2	Bad Company	Ryloth 12	0+	2,000	4,000	6,000
Act 2	Scrapyard Scrap	Ryloth 13	270+ seconds	< 270 sec.	< 180 sec.	< 90 sec.
Act 3	Distraction Action	Behpour 1	0+	2,500	5,000	7,500
Act 3	Low Profile	Behpour 2	0+	1,500	3,000	4,500
Act 3	First Line of Advance	Behpour 3	0+	1,500	3,000	4,500
Act 3	Open Up	Behpour 4	0+	2,000	4,000	6,000
Act 3	Zero Hour	Behpour 5	0+	2,500	5,000	7,500
Act 3	Exit Clearance	Behpour 6	0+	3,750	7,500	11,250
Act 3	A Skywalker Plan	Behpour 7	0+	3,750	7,500	11,250
Act 3	Old Friends	Behpour 8	270+ seconds	< 270 sec.	< 180 sec.	< 90 sec.
Act 3	Old Enemies	Behpour 9	270+ seconds	< 270 sec.	< 180 sec.	< 90 sec.
Act 3	Seconds to Zero	Behpour 10	0+	500	1,000	1,500

Artifacts

Artifacts unlock special entries in your database, and collecting a certain amount of them also unlocks special cheats!

TIP

For specific artifact locations, either find them in the walkthrough or locate them on the maps before each mission.

Act	Mission Name	Mission No.	Artifact Total	Artifact 1	Database Unlockable	Artifact 2	Database Unlockable
Prologue	Master and Padawan	Ryloth 1	0	—	—	—	—
Act 1	Powering up Resdin	Ryloth 2	1	1	Battle Droid	—	—
Act 1	Outpost Initiation	Ryloth 3	3	2	Kano	20	Super
Act 1	Rookie Rendezvous	Ryloth 4	1	3	STAP	—	—
Act 1	Assault!	Juma-9 1	2	4	Frigate	5	Y-Wing
Act 1	Power Reroute	Juma-9 2	1	6	Clone Blaster	—	—
Act 1	Hazardous Infestation	Juma-9 3	2	7	Chameleon	8	Plo
Act 1	Seek and Destroy	Ryloth 5	2	9	Grenade Super	10	Spider
Act 1	Emergency Evac	Ryloth 6	1	11	AAT	—	—
Act 1	Out on Patrol	Ryloth 7	1	12	Rex	—	—
Act 1	Missing in Action	Ryloth 8	2	13	Magna Guard	14	Energy Staff
Act 1	S.O.S.	Juma-9 4	1	15	—	—	—

Act	Mission Name	Mission No.	Artifact Total	Artifact 1	Database Unlockable	Artifact 2	Database Unlockable
Act 1	Abandon Ship!	Juma-9 5	1	16	Mini-Gun	—	—
Act 1	My Name Is Kul Teska	Juma-9 6	0	—	—	—	—
Act 2	Cliff Top	Azloc III 1	1	17	AT-TE	—	—
Act 2	Ground Zero	Azloc III 2	2	18	Aayla	19	Bly
Act 2	Take It Back	Juma-9 7	2	22	Mace Windu	23	Destroyer
Act 2	Inside Out	Juma-9 8	1	24	Emp Grenade	—	—
Act 2	Eye of the Storm	Azloc III 3	2	25	Gree	26	Luminara
Act 2	Guard Duty	Azloc III 4	1	27	Ventress	—	—
Act 2	It's a Trap	Azloc III 5	0	—	—	—	—
Act 2	Enemies of My Enemies	Ryloth 9	1	28	Boomer	—	—
Act 2	Reunion under Fire	Ryloth 10	2	29	Cad Bane	30	Octuptarra
Act 2	Cover Fire	Ryloth 11	1	31	Rocket Launcher	—	—
Act 2	Anybody out There?	Juma-9 9	2	32	Droid Blaster	33	Kit Fisto
Act 2	Rescue Mission	Juma-9 10	2	34	Cody	35	Ponds
Act 2	Vital Escort	Juma-9 11	3	36	Switch	21	Vulture
Act 2	Returning the Favor	Juma-9 12	1	37	Sidious	—	—
Act 2	Bad Company	Ryloth 12	1	38	Kul Teska	—	—
Act 2	Scrapyard Scrap	Ryloth 13	0	—	—	—	—
Act 3	Distraction Action	Behpour 1	2	39	ATRT	40	—
Act 3	Low Profile	Behpour 2	2	41	Obi-Wan	42	Anakin
Act 3	First Line of Advance	Bephour 3	1	43	Ahsoka	—	—
Act 3	Open Up	Behpour 4	2	44	Sabotage	45	Destroyer
Act 3	Zero Hour	Behpour 5	2	46	Crab	47	LAAT
Act 3	Exit Clearance	Behpour 6	1	48	Dooku	—	—
Act 3	A Skywalker Plan	Behpour 7	1	49	Padme	—	—
Act 3	Old Friends	Behpour 8	0	—	—	—	—
Act 3	Old Enemies	Behpour 9	0	—	—	—	—
Act 3	Seconds to Zero	Behpour 10	1	50	Twilight	—	—

Artifact Unlockables

Artifacts Required	Unlockable
5	Jar Jar Eyes/Ears
15	Yoda Hat
25	Big Head Cheat
35	Disco Lights Cheat
50	Darth Vader Head

The Shop

The items listed below can be purchased from the Shop option.

Hat or Mask	Unlockable	Description	PSP Cost	Wii Cost	Next Gen Cost
	Threepio Head	C-3PO's golden head; from Star Wars EP IV: A New Hope	Not on PSP	5,000 Force points	3 artifacts required to unlock
	Boss (Delta Squad)	Boss [RC-1138] Republic Commando helmet; from Star Wars: Republic Commando Game	Not on PSP	5,000 Force points	500 Force points
	Fixer (Delta Squad)	Fixer [RC-1140] Republic Commando helmet; from Star Wars: Republic Commando Game	Not on PSP	5,000 Force points	500 Force points
	Scorch (Delta Squad)	Scorch [RC-1262] Republic Commando helmet; from Star Wars: Republic Commando Game	Not on PSP	5,000 Force points	500 Force points
	Sec (Delta Squad)	Sev [RC-1207] Republic Commando helmet; from Star Wars: Republic Commando Game	Not on PSP	5,000 Force points	500 Force points
	Rota the Huttlet Mask	Rota the Huttlet. "Stinky," Jabba's little bubba; from the Clone Wars	Not on PSP	5,000 Force points	500 Force points
	Gha Nachkt Head	Trandoshan scavenger head; from the Clone Wars	Not on PSP	5,000 Force points	500 Force points
	Ackbar Head	Admiral "It's a trap!" Ackbar head; from Star Wars EP VI: Return of the Jedi	Not on PSP	5,000 Force points	1,000 Force points
	Boba Fett Helmet	Boba Fett helmet; from Star Wars EP V: The Empire Strikes Back	Not on PSP	5,000 Force points	1,000 Force points
	EG-05 Helmet	Lightsaber droid head; from the Clone Wars: Lightsaber Duels game	Not on PSP	5,000 Force points	1,000 Force points
	Greedo Head	Greedo head; everyone's favorite Rodian; from Star Wars EP IV: A New Hope	Not on PSP	5,000 Force points	1,000 Force points
	Imperial Stormtrooper	Imperial stormtrooper helmet; from Star Wars EP IV: A New Hope	Not on PSP	1,000 Force points	1,000 Force points
	Shadow Trooper	Shadow trooper helmet; from Star Wars: The Force Unleashed game	Not on PSP	1,000 Force points	1,000 Force points
	Ithorian	Ithorian head; from Star Wars EP I: The Phantom Menace	Not on PSP	1,000 Force points	1,000 Force points
	Jawa Head	Jawa head; from Star Wars EP IV: A New Hope	Not on PSP	1,000 Force points	1,000 Force points
	Leia Hair Buns	Princess Leia hair buns; from Star Wars EP IV: A New Hope	Not on PSP	5,000 Force points	500 Force points
	Jar Jar Binks Head	Jar Jar head; from Star Wars EP I: The Phantom Menace	Not on PSP	5,000 Force points	Not on Next Gen
	Tusken Raider Head	Tusken Raider head; from Star Wars EP IV: A New Hope	Not on PSP	2,000 Force points	1,000 Force points
	Yoda Head	Yoda head; from Star Wars EP V: The Empire Strikes Back	Not on PSP	5,000 Force points	15 artifacts required to unlock
	Emperor Head	Hooded emperor head; from Star Wars EP VI: Return of the Jedi	Not on PSP	5,000 Force points	1,500 Force points
	Commando Droid Mask	Commando droid head; from the Clone Wars	Not on PSP	1,000 Force points	1,500 Force points
	Indy Hat	Sable brown fedora, as worn by Indiana Jones	Not on PSP	5,000 Force points	2,000 Force points

Hats and Masks

Hat or Mask	Unlockable	Description	PSP Cost	Wii Cost	Next Gen Cost
	Bane's Hat	Cad Bane's hat; from the Clone Wars	Not on PSP	5,000 Force points	1,000 Force points
	Wookiee Head	Wookiee head, as seen on Chewbacca in Star Wars EP IV: A New Hope	Not on PSP	5,000 Force points	1,500 Force points
	Darth Maul Head	Darth Maul head; from Star Wars EP I: The Phantom Menace	Not on PSP	5,000 Force points	1,500 Force points
	Darth Vader Head	Darth Vader mask; from Star Wars EP IV: A New Hope	Not on PSP	5,000 Force points	50 artifacts required to unlock
	Grievous Mask	General Grievous mask; from the Clone Wars	Not on PSP	5,000 Force points	1,500 Force points
	Teska's Head	Kul Teska's head; from this game!	Not on PSP	3,000 Force points	2,000 Force points
	Bith Musician Head	Clone Wars–styled Bith head; cantina musician from Star Wars EP IV: A New Hope	Not on PSP	5,000 Force points	1,000 Force points

Combat Upgrades

Upgrade	Applies to	Description	PSP Cost	Wii Cost	Next Gen Cost
Combo Master	Jedi	Longer combo cooldown	5,000 Force points	10,000 Force points	4,500 Force points
Steady Hand	Clone	Extra damage from crouch shots	5,000 Force points	8,000 Force points	4,000 Force points
Pack Rat	Clone	Double max secondary weapon capacity	5,000 Force points	5,000 Force points	4,000 Force points
Ace Pilot	Clone	Cause extra damage when riding vehicles	10,000 Force points	10,000 Force points	4,000 Force points
Force Push	Jedi	Wider Force Push. Faster to charge	10,000 Force points	5,000 Force points	4,000 Force points
Lightsaber Throw	Jedi	Spins around body twice in widening circle	20,000 Force points	3,500 Force points	4,500 Force points
Force Kill	Jedi	Larger shock wave on Force Kill	20,000 Force points	10,000 Force points	4,500 Force points
Jump Attack	Jedi	Larger shock wave on jump attack	20,000 Force points	10,000 Force points	4,500 Force points

Droid-Jack Upgrades

Upgrade	Description	PSP Cost	Wii Cost	Next Gen Cost
Super Battle Droid	Stay on longer	20,000 Force points	10,000 Force points	5,000 Force points
Spider Droid	More shots	10,000 Force points	6,000 Force points	5,000 Force points
Destroyer Droid	Go farther. Take more damage	10,000 Force points	6,000 Force points	5,000 Force points
Chameleon Droid	Lay more mines	10,000 Force points	6,000 Force points	5,000 Force points
Crab Droid	Do more stomps	20,000 Force points	8,000 Force points	5,000 Force points
Sabotage Droid	Do more damage	20,000 Force points	8,000 Force points	5,000 Force points
Magna Guard	Stay on longer	20,000 Force points	10,000 Force points	5,000 Force points

Droid Dances

Droid	Dance	PSP Cost	Wii Cost	Next Gen Cost
Battle Droid	Step-Stop-Bop!	Not on PSP	10,000 Force points	2,500 Force points
Super Battle Droid	Kalinka Clanker	Not on PSP	10,000 Force points	2,500 Force points
Spider Droid	Busta Move!	Not on PSP	10,000 Force points	2,500 Force points
Destroyer Droid	Rollin' 'n' Rockin'!	Not on PSP	10,000 Force points	2,500 Force points
Chameleon Droid	Everybody Dance Now!	Not on PSP	10,000 Force points	2,500 Force points
Crab Droid	Get Down Crab Style!	Not on PSP	10,000 Force points	2,500 Force points
Sabotage Droid	Spin, Twirl, and Groove!	Not on PSP	10,000 Force points	2,500 Force points
Magna Guard	Heavy Metal Strut	Not on PSP	10,000 Force points	2,500 Force points

Cheats

Unlockable	Description	PSP Cost	Wii Cost	Next Gen Cost
Big Heads Mode	Characters have BIG heads	Not on PSP	10,000 Force points	25 artifacts to unlock
Weapon Light Show	Blaster fire brightness increased	Not on PSP	Not on Wii	35 artifacts to unlock
Thermal Detonator	Infinite thermal detonators	20,000 Force points	20,000 Force points	15,000 Force points
Rocket Launcher	Infinite rockets for the rocket launcher	20,000 Force points	20,000 Force points	15,000 Force points
Minigun	Infinite ammo for the minigun	Not on PSP	20,000 Force points	15,000 Force points
Extra Damage	Continuous extra damage	20,000 Force points	10,000 Force points	20,000 Force points
Combo Bar	Continuous full Combo bar	30,000 Force points	10,000 Force points	20,000 Force points
Force Blast	Continuous Force Blast ability	10,000 Force points	30,000 Force points	200,000 Force points
Ultimate Lightsaber	Obliterate every target in one hit	180,000 Force points	40,000 Force points	100,000 Force points
Invulnerability	Continuous invulnerability	200,000 Force points	40,000 Force points	100,000 Force points

Achievements and Trophies

The following is a list of all Xbox 360 Achievements and PS3 Trophies.

#	Name	How to Achieve	Type	PS3 Trophy Type	Xbox 360 Gamerpoints	Notes and Tips
1	Refresher Course	Complete the prologue mission, "Master and Padawan"	Mission	Bronze	10	

#	Name	How to Achieve	Type	PS3 Trophy Type	Xbox 360 Gamerpoints	Notes and Tips
2	Act 1 Padawan	Complete all Act 1 missions on Padawan difficulty	Mission	Bronze	10	—
3	Act 1 Master	Complete all Act 1 missions on Master difficulty	Mission	Bronze	15	—
4	Act 2 Padawan	Complete all Act 2 missions on Padawan difficulty	Mission	Bronze	10	—
5	Act 2 Master	Complete all Act 2 missions on Master difficulty	Mission	Bronze	15	—
6	Act 3 Padawan	Complete all Act 3 missions on Padawan difficulty	Mission	Silver	30	—
7	Act 3 Master	Complete all Act 3 missions on Master difficulty	Mission	Gold	90	—
8	Republic Heroes	Complete all missions with another player	Mission Special	Silver	30	—
9	Youngling Award	Get at least a Bronze medal for every challenge	Challenge	Bronze	15	—
10	Master Award	Get a Gold medal for every challenge	Challenge	Silver	30	—
11	Jawa Scavenger	Collect 1 artifact	Artifact	Bronze	10	See "Jawa Lord"
12	Jawa Hunter	Collect 25 artifacts	Artifact	Bronze	10	See "Jawa Lord"
13	Jawa Lord	Collect 50 artifacts	Artifact	Silver	30	Use the maps before each mission or use the artifact table to locate all 50 artifacts.
14	Come Back Soon	Buy a costume	Shop	Bronze	10	—
15	Combat Master	Buy all Combat upgrades	Shop	Bronze	15	—
16	Droid Master	Buy all Droid Control upgrades	Shop	Bronze	15	—
17	Dance Master	Buy all Droid Dancing upgrades	Shop	Bronze	15	—
18	Dressed for Success	Buy every costume	Shop	Silver	30	—
19	Jedi Knight	Get a Gold medal on a Jedi mission	Medal	Bronze	15	See the "Mission Rank" table in the "Unlockables" chapter.
20	Clone Captain	Get a Gold medal on a clone mission	Medal	Bronze	15	See the "Mission Rank" table in the "Unlockables" chapter.
21	Jedi Master	Get a Platinum medal on a Jedi mission	Medal	Bronze	15	See the "Mission Rank" table in the "Unlockables" chapter.
22	Clone Commander	Get a Platinum medal on a clone mission	Medal	Bronze	15	See the "Mission Rank" table in the "Unlockables" chapter.
23	Girl Power	Complete all Jedi missions as Ahsoka	Character	Bronze	15	—
24	Nobody Messes With...	Complete all clone missions as Cad Bane	Character	Silver	30	—
25	Two's Company	Complete a mission with another player	Mission Special	Bronze	10	—
26	Dynamic Duo	Complete all Jedi missions as Anakin and Ahsoka	Character	Bronze	15	—
27	Heroic Alliance	Finish a mission in Co-op mode with a combined score of over 10,000 points	Mission Special	Bronze	15	—

#	Name	How to Achieve	Type	PS3 Trophy Type	Xbox 360 Gamerpoints	Notes and Tips
28	High Achiever	Get a combined top score for all missions over 200,000 points	Mission Special	Silver	30	—
29	Time to kill	Get a combined best time for all missions under 200 minutes	Mission Special	Silver	30	—
30	Scrap Lord	Destroy over 5,000 droids	Feat	Silver	30	—
31	Droid Disruptor	Get over 250 points with a single droid-jack	Droid-Jack	Bronze	10	—
32	Demolition Derby	Destroy over 100 droids with droid-jacks	Droid-Jack	Bronze	15	—
33	Droid Dynamo	Get over 100 points with each type of droid-jack	Droid-Jack	Bronze	15	—
34	Double Trouble	Control a droid at the same time another player is controlling a droid	Droid-Jack	Bronze	10	Droid-jack one droid while your partner jacks another.
35	Kill Joy	Push a Co-op partner off edges 10 times	Feat	Bronze	15	—
36	Dance of Death	Destroy 25 droids while they are dancing	Feat	Bronze	15	You must first purchase the Dancing Droids cheats to accomplish this feat.
37	Bowling Master	Destroy 10 droids with a rolling destroyer	Droid-Jack	Bronze	15	—
38	My Hero	Destroy 10 droids that are attacking your partner	Feat	Bronze	15	—
39	Grand Slam	Destroy 25 droids by doing a jump attack off another player	Feat	Bronze	15	—
40	Multi-Mayhem Master	Perform 10 of each multikill feat	Feat	Silver	30	—
41	Handle with Care	Destroy 20 droids with an explosive prop	Feat	Bronze	15	—
42	Up Close and Personal	Destroy 50 droids with a clone melee attack	Feat	Bronze	15	Kill 10 enemies by doing a jump attack off an ally.
43	Force Crusher	Destroy 50 droids with a mounted Force Kill	Feat	Bronze	15	—
44	Watch Your Step	Push 50 enemies off an edge to their doom	Feat	Bronze	15	—
45	Tag Team	Destroy 100 droids your partner has stunned	Feat	Bronze	15	This can be easily accomplished while your partner droid-jacks an enemy and weakens the other droids.
46	Gold Leader	Force Kill one of each type of gold droid	Feat	Bronze	15	—
47	I Got One!	Destroy a gold droid	Feat	Bronze	10	—
48	No Favorites	Destroy at least one droid while controlling each type of droid	Droid-Jack	Bronze	15	Droid-jack every type of droid and destroy another.
49	Can't Touch Me	Defeat Kul Teska without either player dying	Character	Bronze	15	—
50	Campaign Veteran	Get a Gold medal for every mission	Medal	Gold	90	See "Jawa Lord"

THE ART OF REPUBLIC HEROES

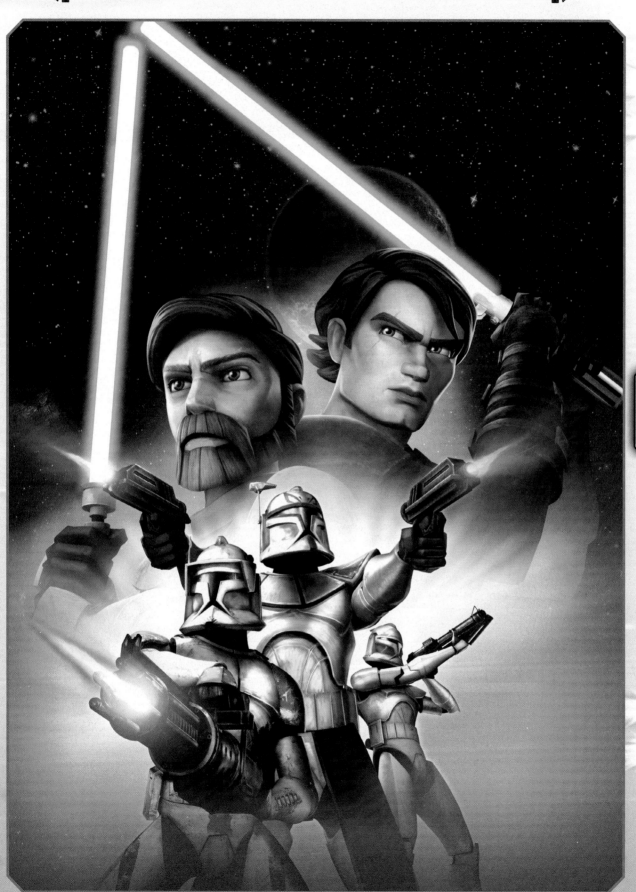

Azloc III

ALZOC 3
ADAM NICHOLS

TEXTURES REQUIRED:

ADAM
NICHOLS
2008

ALZOC
DOME

1X ICE SHELF - 512X1024
1X SCROLLING CLOUDS - 256X256
1X STARS - 128X128
1X MOON - 128X128
1X GENERIC WHITE 32X32

STAR WARS
THE
CLONE
WARS
REPUBLIC HEROES

PRIMA OFFICIAL GAME GUIDE

Bephour

BEPHOUR - HIGH LEVEL - WEAPON TIME - CONE

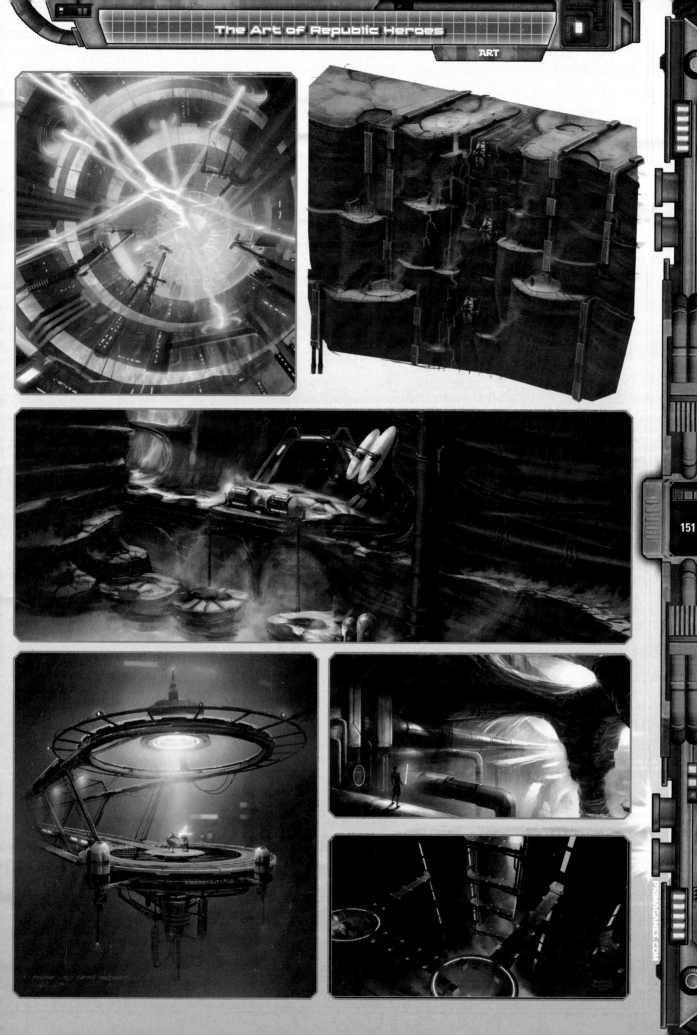

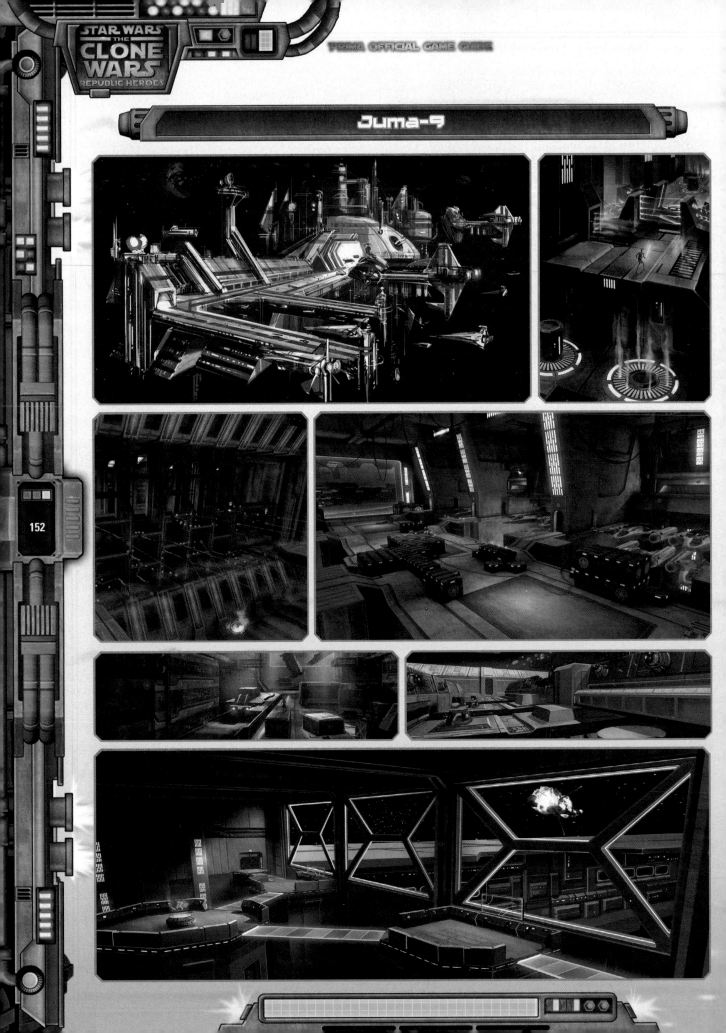

ART

CH. 09 - SSI CORRIDOR BLOCKER - #1

ACT 2 - STAP CHASE UP ELEVATOR SHAFT

Ryloth

Characters

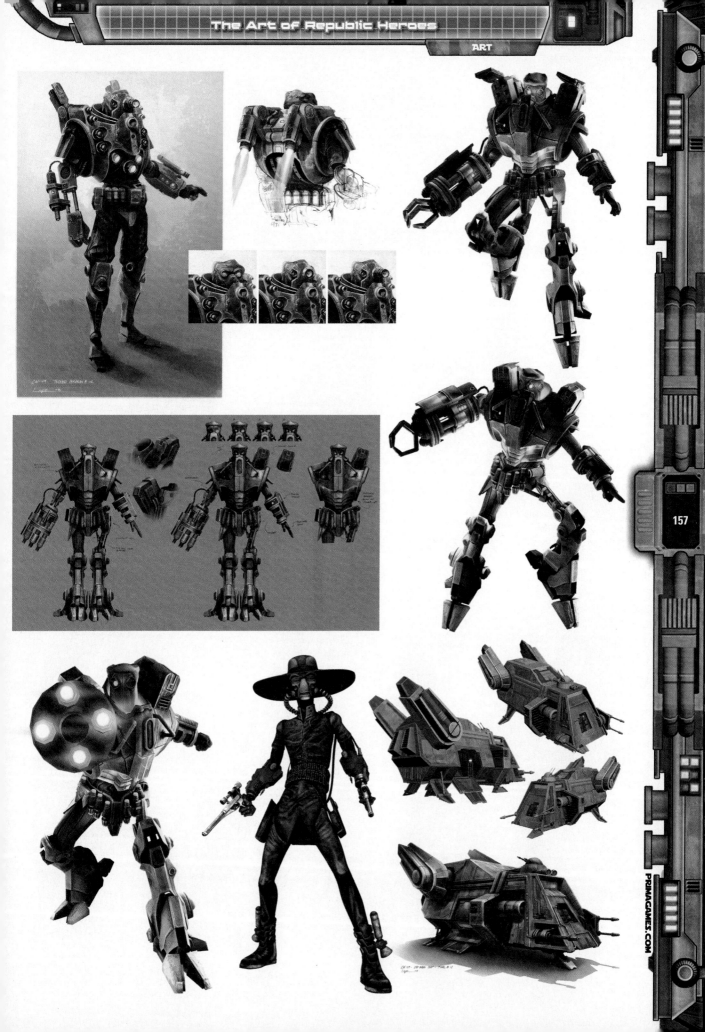